6-20-2006

Rich,

This book contains a number of the pieces I remember most from my years as a writer and an editor.

I wanted you to have this— in appreciation for everything you have done for me at Sartell Golf Club.

Please know that I wish the best for you always, and I hope you will enjoy the book.

Michael Larson

There's Magic All Around Us

There's Magic All Around Us

✦

Powerful stories to help you live a fuller life

Michael Larson

iUniverse, Inc.
New York Lincoln Shanghai

There's Magic All Around Us
Powerful stories to help you live a fuller life

iUniverse books may be ordered through booksellers or by contacting:

iUniverse
2021 Pine Lake Road, Suite 100
Lincoln, NE 68512
www.iuniverse.com
1-800-Authors (1-800-288-4677)

ISBN-13: 978-0-595-39004-5 (pbk)
ISBN-13: 978-0-595-83417-4 (cloth)
ISBN-13: 978-0-595-83395-5 (ebk)
ISBN-10: 0-595-39004-8 (pbk)
ISBN-10: 0-595-83417-5 (cloth)
ISBN-10: 0-595-83395-0 (ebk)

Printed in the United States of America

This book is dedicated to my mother, Lois Holte Larson, who has always been my most loyal fan, and to my father, Leonard O. Larson, who always seemed to believe I could do no wrong.

My mother still lives on the Long Lake farm six miles south of St. James, Minn., where I grew up.

My father died in 1985 at the age of 75. I wish we could have another catch, Dad.

Contents

Foreword

I have always wanted to be a journalist.

Even as a boy, I would get my mother to drive me into town to pick up sheets of newsprint at the local weekly newspaper shop. Back home with these sheets, I would sit at the kitchen table or at the desk in my bedroom, creating newspapers and magazines. I wrote such scintillating prose as, "My grandpa tells me he can't let his sheep get sick. My grandpa says a sick sheep is a dead sheep." In some cases, I would make extra copies of my publications and send them to my aunts and uncles and suggest that they might want to subscribe—at a reasonable rate, of course.

As a third-quarter sophomore at the University of Minnesota and wandering aimlessly into various courses, still not quite sure what I wanted to be when I grew up, I can remember walking by Murphy Hall and seeing the large capital letters above the high arched brick doorways proclaiming "SCHOOL OF JOURNALISM." "That's what I've always wanted to do," I remember thinking to myself. "That's what I should do." I walked into the building, found one of the professors, and spent the next 35 years of my life carving out a career in journalism.

In putting together this book of my writings, I decided to break the pieces into seasons, either because a piece was written during a certain season or because its topic seemed to fit into a certain season. I did add one more category, "Seasons," for those pieces that didn't fit easily into "Spring," "Summer," "Autumn," or "Winter." Five sections. Call me egotistical, but I figured if William Shakespeare could write his plays in five acts, I could put together a book with five parts.

I've always considered myself a very positive person. To paraphrase the cliché, I always tend to see the glass of water as at least half full. As a young man, I read Norman Vincent Peale's best-selling book, "The Power of Positive Thinking," and to this day, I still credit him for enhancing my outlook on life.

"One of the most important and powerful facts about you," Peale writes, "is expressed in the following statement by William James, who was one of the wisest men America has produced. William James said, 'The greatest discovery of my generation *is that human beings can alter their lives by altering their attitudes of mind.*' As you think, so shall you be. So flush out all old, tired, worn-out thoughts. Fill your mind with fresh, new creative thoughts of faith, love and goodness. By this process, you can actually remake your life."

In this book, you will meet some people who have gone way beyond my level of positive thinking.

It continues to amaze me how incredibly some people can deal with adversity. Even in situations where they are facing tragic situations, even the worst things we can imagine, they draw upon reserves of emotional and spiritual strength that stagger the imagination.

The first two pieces in this book demonstrate this incredible capacity to deal with life and death, even when it seems incredibly unfair.

In addition to writing articles that demonstrate such strength, it has been my intent here to offer pieces of writing that inspire, that force deep thought, that beg for empathy, that bring a smile to your face or that might even bring you to tears. Throughout this book, I hope you will find a thread showing the incredible courage, persistence, love, hope and the wonder that's all-present in this marvelous world of which we all are a part.

When you have finished reading, I hope you will agree with me that there really is magic all around us.

—Michael Larson

Seasons

o o o o o o o o o o o o o o o o o o o o o o o o o o o o o o

Four Seasons fill the measure of the year;
There are four seasons in the mind of man:
He has his lusty Spring, when fancy clear
Takes in all beauty with an easy span:
He has his Summer, when luxuriously
Spring's honied cud of youthful thought he loves
To ruminate, and by such dreaming high
Is nearest unto heaven: quiet coves
His soul has in its Autumn, when his wings
He furleth close; contented so to look
On mists in idleness—to let fair things
Pass by unheeded as a threshold brook.
He has his Winter, too, of pale misfeature,
Or else he would forego his mortal nature

To every thing there is a season, and a time to every purpose under the heaven.

—John Keats
"The Human Seasons"

She's in heaven now

—First published on Jan. 8, 1980

"I'll lend you for a little time
A child of mine," he said.
"For you to love the while she lives
And mourn for when she's dead.
It may be six or seven years
Or twenty-two or three.
But will you, till I call her back,
Take care of her for me?
She'll bring her charms to gladden you,
And should her stay be brief,
You'll have her lovely memories
As solace for your grief."

■

Kelly Ann Carlson was just 2½ years old when her parents discovered she had leukemia.

"I thought she had a cold," remembers her mother, Christine. "She had a small fever for a couple of days."

Dale and Christine, with daughters Kelly and Heather, had traveled to North Mankato to visit Christine's mother, Vivian Hensel. That day, Kelly's temperature rose to 104 degrees.

The Carlsons rushed her to the emergency room at St. Joseph's Hospital. There, a Rochester doctor whose specialty was leukemia noticed symptoms of the disease in Kelly.

A blood test confirmed the diagnosis.

That was on Oct. 28. "By 10 p.m., we were on our way to Rochester," Dale said.

At St. Marys Hospital, further tests showed Kelly's white blood count was dangerously high, 230,000 to 240,000 cells per cubic millimeter of blood, compared to the normal count of 5,000 to 10,000.

Kelly was diagnosed to have ALL, acute lymphocytic leukemia.

The diagnosis stunned both Christine and Dale.

"It doesn't quite seem real," Christine said. For Dale, "It was like, yes, you will wake up from this."

The Carlsons had no medical insurance. But at the hospital, they learned about state and federal funds administered through the Crippled Children's Fund; that would help them pay for Kelly's medical care.

As for Kelly, "she really didn't understand what was going on," Christine said. "She was really good, though. She never really cried."

The doctors treating her would "explain to Kelly what they were going to do. She was only 2 years old, but I think it helped."

■

"I cannot promise she will stay,
Since all from earth return,
But there are lessons taught down there,
I want this child to learn.
I've looked this wide world over
In my search for teachers true,
And from the throngs that crowd life's lanes,
I have selected you;
Now will you give her all your love,
Not think the labor vain,
Nor hate me when I come to call
And take her back again."

■

Kelly was placed in intensive care at St. Marys. She responded to treatment so quickly that she was moved into a private room.

Five days later, on Nov. 2, Kelly was back home with her family, in the farm house they rent at Route 1, Butterfield.

The next day, however, "she really didn't want to do anything," her mother said. "She just sat around."

Kelly had been scheduled to undergo chemotherapy treatments every Monday, Wednesday and Friday at nearby St. James.

But by that Monday, Nov. 5, her temperature had soared again, this time to 106 degrees.

The Carlsons rushed Kelly back to Rochester, and again she was placed in intensive care.

Doctors at Rochester explained that treatments designed to slow the multiplication of white blood cells also had lowered Kelly's ability to fight germs. A germ already in her body had caused an infection in her blood system.

During the next week, the doctors struggled to save Kelly—transfusions to stabilize her blood count, antibiotics to stop her infection.

But the struggle would fall short.

On Nov. 14, Kelly told her mother, "I'm going to go night-night now." She woke up several times during the night and talked to her parents and to Dale's mother. All of them were by her bedside.

About midnight, Kelly opened her eyes, looked at her mother, and said, "Bye, Mom."

At 6:05 a.m. on Nov. 14, Kelly died.

"It was not that she was in pain," Dale said. "She just kept getting weaker and weaker."

The loss of the little girl hit the Carlsons deeply.

"If it wasn't for your faith in God," Dale said, "it would be pretty tough to pull out of one of these things.

"Our families were great through the whole thing, though—and our friends, a lot of support."

Also great during the ordeal, her parents said, was Kelly.

"She was super good," Dale said. When doctors would finish taking a blood sample from her, she would just say, "All done."

"Sometimes," Christine said, "you wanted to say, 'Stop poking her.'"

But now, her mother says, Kelly doesn't have to go through any more of that.

Dale explains, "It's kind of like, now it's over for her. She's in heaven, and now she understands."

■

I fancied that I heard them say,
"Dear Lord, Thy will be done,
For all the joy the child shall bring,
The risk of grief we'll run.
We'll shelter her with tenderness,
We'll love her while we may,
And for the happiness we've known
Forever grateful stay.
But should the angels call for her
Much sooner than we planned,
We'll brave the bitter grief that comes,
And try to understand."

—Poem read at Kelly's funeral
Nov. 21, 1979

Guest poem helps us all

—Condensed from columns published on Feb. 7 and Feb. 14 in 1980

"I can't tell you how that article about Kelly Ann hit me," the Mankato woman was saying over the phone.

The woman, who asked that her name not be used, had called because she had just read about Kelly Ann Carlson, the 2-year-old girl from Butterfield, Minn., featured in a column Jan. 8. Kelly, the daughter of Christine and Dale Carlson, died of leukemia last November.

The story of Kelly affected her deeply, the woman continued, because her grandson had died when he was just four months old.

"It was crib death," she said.

The woman began explaining that her daughter had been in and out of trouble while growing up.

Later, the daughter had enrolled in a Job Corps program, and while in that program, she had met Robert F. Kennedy. She had talked with him. She had listened to his words. And when she was able to absorb those words, the Mankato woman said, her daughter became a changed person.

"She straightened her life out."

The woman and her daughter had been living in the same home when the boy died.

The daughter and her family, including two girls and the boy, were living upstairs. The mother was living downstairs.

"I'll never forget her screaming," the woman said, when her daughter discovered the boy had stopped breathing.

"'Mother, help me!' she was screaming."

Both mother and daughter tried to revive the baby.

"Then the firemen came. They got him to breathe again, but his little heart just gave out."

The boy had died on Nov. 22, 1977.

Nov. 22, the same day John F. Kennedy had died in 1963, the Mankato woman said.

The date was significant for her—the link between John F. Kennedy and Robert F. Kennedy and her daughter, the reason she had mentioned how the late senator had turned her daughter's life around.

The death of the boy had been devastating for both the Mankato woman and her daughter.

A program at Children's Hospital in St. Paul had provided much help for both of them, she said. Children's Hospital offers a special program for relatives of children who have died of "crib death," or sudden infant death syndrome (SIDS).

The program also had helped the daughter's two girls, the woman said.

One of the girls, age 3, had become "very mean after her brother died." Among other things, she would beat on her dolls and pull their hair. Physicians at the hospital explained, "That was her way of showing her grief for her brother."

Another woman, Kathy Hoppes, also called about the column about Kelly. She provided valuable information, saying that the poem read at Kelly's funeral is called "To All Parents." The author is Edgar A. Guest.

When Mrs. Hoppes worked at a hospital in Lincoln, Neb., the poem always was sent from the staff on her floor to the survivors of patients who had died.

"The poem helps the parents of small children a lot," she says. "But, really, it's a poem that helps anyone when someone close to them has died."

There are different versions of the poem, Mrs. Hoppes said. She sent along her copy, saying, "There are a few words that are different from the version that appeared [with the Kelly article.]"

Ruby Schmidt of Arlington also supplied the name of the author. She said a copy of the poem had been sent to her "35 years ago in 1945 when my little girl was born. It was a clipping from the paper, and it was written by Edgar A. Guest."

Learning experiences

—First published on March 27, 1980

It's interesting how your memory pops into gear when you run into an old friend.

Newton Moen is an administrator at East High School in Mankato now, but I first knew him when he taught at St. James, Minn. Among other things, he endured me in driver's education classes.

So when we ran across one another at a party, we had time to reminisce.

■ In a driver's education class, Moen lifted the hood of our car, pointed to an object and asked a girl in the class to name it. She answered correctly, and I've been thankful ever since. I had no clue. How embarrassing it would have been to publicly admit I didn't recognize the car's horn.

■ Waiting for a driver's education class to begin, some of us were skipping pebbles across Armstrong Boulevard. One of my pebbles hopped up under a passing car; the driver stopped and took my name (I didn't think fast enough to come up with a false one). During class a few days later, Moen said, "I hear you've been throwing rocks at cars. I trust you won't do that again." He didn't have to say more.

■ I flunked my driver's exam on the first try. Moen seemed surprised. But in class, he had told us not to take the corners too slowly, that the testers would mark you off for that. So I sped around the turns, and my tester never said a word about me going too slowly; however, he did suggest I might want to cool it on corners when I took my test for the second time. I found out later that Moen meant his suggestion primarily for the girl drivers, who tended to be timid when they took their corners.

My driving test had started poorly anyway. I nearly flipped the tester into the back seat when we squealed out from the curb where the car was parked. The driving tester had made some opening remarks, then told me to pull out. I had the accelerator halfway to the floor when I realized the parking brake was on. I released it without thinking to lift my foot, and we screeched into the street.

While talking with Moen, other learning experiences popped back into my brain:

■ Listening to a comedy record at home one evening, I decided it might be adapted into a dandy piece for my senior English class. It was a hit with the teacher—She even read it aloud in front of the class. I didn't worry right away. But when a classmate began reciting some of the lines to a friend of ours, and that friend said, "I think I heard something like that on a record somewhere," no one had to give me any more lessons about plagiarism.

■ Several junior high students were standing beneath an eighth-grade classroom, flipping a dead pigeon toward an open window on the second floor. Their tries were falling short or going wide. On one of the misses, I scrambled to retrieve the pigeon, saying, "Give me that." I proceeded to wind up, and I threw the pigeon right through the open window, into the classroom. Unfortunately, the school athletic director was walking by at the time and he saw everything. That adventure ended with me taking a trip to the eighth-grade classroom to apologize to the teacher and to the pupils in his room.

■ When our history teacher asked for six volunteers to debate the candidacies of Richard Nixon and John Kennedy, I ended up on the Kennedy team. Our teacher said we would poll the class before the debate to gauge the Nixon-Kennedy sentiment in our class. She said we would vote again after the debate. I leaned over to one of my best friends, who also would be debating for Kennedy, and said, "Vote for Nixon." After the debate, both of us voted for Kennedy. We weren't terribly surprised when the teacher said the Kennedy side had done very well—it had picked up two votes.

Just think positive

—First published on March 19, 1981

His picture is there on page 6 of the high school yearbook, the man who first helped me believe that the mind rules the body.

Eugene Auringer was our chemistry instructor at St. James High School.

He often talked about physical conditioning, and he often talked about mind power. There were times, he said, when he would wake up and feel weak; his stomach might not feel just right, and he might think the flu was coming on.

At times like that, he said, you must talk to your body. You must tell it to stay well. Usually, he said, the technique brings success.

Ever since I heard Auringer's words, I've found his advice almost always works for me. And even though some people insist it's just so much imagination, there are a lot of us carrying the torch for mind over sickness.

What brought Auringer's theory back to mind was a Dale Carnegie "positive thinking" book I picked up at the Minnesota Valley Regional Library's last used-book sale.

Carnegie, discussing worry, noted that "it took medical science 2,300 years to recognize this great truth. We are just now beginning to develop a new kind of medicine called psychosomatic medicine—a medicine that treats both the mind and the body. It is high time we are doing that, for medical science has largely wiped out the terrible diseases caused by physical germs—diseases such as small-pox, cholera, yellow fever and scores of other scourges that swept untold millions into untimely graves. But medical science has been unable to cope with the mental and physical wrecks caused not by germs, but by emotions of worry, fear, hate, frustration and despair."

Plato once wrote: "The greatest mistake physicians make is that they attempt to cure the body without attempting to cure the mind; yet the mind and body are one and should not be treated separately."

Gen. Ulysses Grant, with his troops attacking Richmond during the Civil War, became ill even as his men were chasing Gen. Robert E. Lee's soldiers from the city.

In his "Memoirs," Gen. Grant recalled that he had developed a violent headache.

"I spent the night in bathing my feet in hot water and mustard plasters on my wrists and the back part of my neck, hoping to be cured by morning," he wrote.

The next morning, a horseman rode up carrying a letter of surrender from Gen. Lee.

"When the officer [bearing the message] reached me," Gen. Grant said, "I was still suffering with the sick headache; but the instant I saw the contents of the note, I was cured."

Doctors at the University of Minnesota Hospitals in Minneapolis have been teaching children to use self-hypnosis to relieve problems such as asthma, headaches, abdominal pain and vomiting.

Pediatric psychologist Pi-Nian Chang explained that the self-hypnosis technique assumes that people make themselves tense; therefore, people also can learn to make themselves relax.

The method has worked especially well with children ages 5 to 8—they have vivid imaginations and few misconceptions, Chang said.

In Chang's program, children are taught to concentrate, to relax each part of the body, to paint visual images of what they want to accomplish. Once relaxed, the children are able to persuade the body to open bronchial tubes, to unclench abdominal muscles and to make headaches disappear.

Chang said no one knows how the method works neurologically. But the important point, he said, is that it does work.

It stands to reason that if youngsters using self-hypnosis can learn to erase pain, the rest of us should be able to use mind power to erase pain, too.

Some years ago in Illinois, I participated in a two-day seminar focusing on a theory called "Silva Mind Control."

During the two-day course, use of the mind was stretched a bit further than I could accept—students were "taught" to use mind control to keep signal lights on green until they could make it through an intersection, for example, and students were taught to "program ahead" for a parking space in a congested area.

But students did tell of using mind control to get over upset stomachs, to eliminate headaches, even to endure pain caused by drilling dentists.

That's not to say that the mind could—or should—be used to cure tooth decay, set a broken bone or dissolve a cancerous tumor. But the number of malingering patients given sugar tablets by their doctors is at least one indicator that often what the mind believes the body can do, the body will do.

A study of 15,000 patients at the Mayo Clinic in Rochester confirmed that theory some years ago.

All the patients complained of stomach ailments. But doctors discovered that four out of every five patients had no physical basis whatever for their stomach illnesses.

That may be why people who exercise well, by running, playing tennis, swimming, biking or walking seem to stay so healthy. They're doing something positive to strengthen both their minds and their bodies.

They're smart enough to know that they can use their minds to show their bodies who is boss.

Sometimes things dangle

—First published on March 11, 1982

My favorite example of imprecise writing appeared in a Southern Minnesota newspaper about 10 years ago.

The newspaper—let's keep it anonymous to preserve its integrity—published an article about a truck driver losing control of his semi and driving it through a restaurant wall in Windom.

A portion of the news report contained the information that "eight people were seated in the restaurant when the truck came crashing through the wall drinking coffee."

The Columbia Journalism Review publishes such examples of imprecision each month.

Now many of the finest flubs have been compiled into a book entitled, *Squad helps dog bite victim.*

The book features misleading headlines, unfortunate juxtapositions of headlines and photographs, misleading photo captions and unintentionally humorous arrangements of words. It's nice change-of-pace reading.

Some of the best offerings:

■ "Chief Blue, the last full-blooded Catawba Indian chief, died in 1959. The *Evening Herald* incorrectly said Wednesday that he died three years ago due to a reporting error."

■ "Bound, gagged and trussed up nude in a denim bag, with plugs in her ears and tape over her eyes, Cleveland teacher Linda L. Sharpe told yesterday how she was kidnapped in Florida, not knowing where she was going or why."

■ "'Our workshop is an attempt to set up an old biddy system to encourage those women who made it the hard way to help the younger women who are trying to move up.'"

■ "The above are sample questions based on the test that Penn State is giving to journalism students in all but one of the professional course. The questions deal only with comma, faults, dangling modifiers, spelling punctuation, and usage. There are no errors in capitalization and there is supposed to be only one error per sentence. Students are cautioned that the error must be viewed in the context of the entire sentence and that rewriting a sentence is not the answer."

■ "In Sunday's *Courier-Express* Rita Smith writes about a teenage prostitute who refuses to change her way of life despite the pleas of her anguished mother. For home delivery, phone 847-5500."

■ "Do you enjoy writing and are looking for helpful criticism to improve?"

■ "One witness told the commissioners that she had seen sexual intercourse taking place between two parked cars in front of her house."

■ "A 14-year-old Ottawa girl told Ottawa police early this morning that while she babysat at a home on Jefferson Street a man tapped on a window, then exposed himself to her, city police said today. Police were able to get only a partial description of the man, officers said."

■ "Arthur Fiedler, the jolly, unsnobbish conductor of the Boston Pops Orchestra, knew just how much tuneful classical music Mr. And Mrs. Average could take. After nearly 50 years of spreading musical joy, he is dead at 84."

■ "The Assembly passed and sent to the Senate a bill requiring dog owners in New York City to clean up after their pets, on penalty of a $100 fine. The bill also applies to Buffalo."

■ "By then she will have shed 80 of the 240 pounds she weighed in with when she entered the Peter Bent Brigham Hospital obesity program. A third of her left behind."

■ "Ken Strachan, editor of the *Brantford Expositor*, spoke at the annual meeting of the Women's Institute on May 17.

"The group decided to make a donation to the Mental Health Association."

■ "After years of being lost under a pile of dust, Walter P. Stanley III found all the old records of the Bangor Lions Club at the Bangor House. On Jan. 18 he donated them in a presentation to Lions Club President Earl Black."

■ "'You couldn't talk to a nicer guy [than Taylor],' said Mrs. Doris Lauer, who lived across the street from the Taylors.

"'You never would have thought he had mental problems,' she said, asking not to be identified."

The editors of the *Columbia Journalism Review* identify the perpetrators of these imprecise passages. Those curious enough will just have to buy the book. There's no reason to embarrass anyone here.

The latest example of imprecise writing appeared last week, again in a Southern Minnesota newspaper—and, again, let's keep it anonymous.

Under a headline that said "Hopefuls Applying to be School Head," the reporter wrote:

"Fourteen applications have been received by the...school district for the position of superintendent of schools, according to the district office.

"None of the applicants are female, so far."

Irish rule in New Ulm

—First published on March 3, 1981

The Irish of New Ulm are determined to wrest this year's St. Patrick's Day celebration back from the Germans.

As Irishman Terry Dempsey sees it, "They did such a mediocre job last year, we just have to take it back from them."

German Don Brand, however, doesn't quite agree. "Last year's may have been the best [St. Patrick's Day] parade ever. We're giving it back to them this year, but they're going to have a hard time topping 1980."

The participation of New Ulm's Germans in the traditional Irish celebration began early last March 17.

Brand, who in addition to leading parades also serves as news director for KNUJ Radio, remembers that on St. Patrick's Day morning, he "called City Hall and asked if anybody had taken out a parade permit."

"They said, no, no one had taken out a parade permit. I said, 'Hell, I'm going to organize a parade.'"

When faithful church-goer Brand utters such an expletive, you know he means business.

"We started this whole thing about 10 o'clock," Brand said, "and by noon, it was pretty well arranged. We broadcast all the details at noon, and we told everybody to meet at 5 o'clock at Second Street and Minnesota."

The caring shown by the Germans over the St. Patrick's Day celebration should not come as a surprise to anyone, Brand said.

The annual parade in New Ulm began in 1965, and the city's Irish residents claim that makes it the longest-running St. Patrick's Day parade in Minnesota—one year longer than St. Paul's.

So when Brand discovered that no parade permit had been taken out, and realized that Dempsey was busy legislating in St. Paul and that William O'Connor, a New Ulm lawyer who also helps organize St. Patrick's Day festivities, was in the hospital, he could see the annual tradition was in trouble.

"We decided the Germans couldn't let a tradition like this die," Brand said, "even if it was for the Irish."

Brand paid for the $2 parade permit himself.

Then he began organizing.

Soon the parade had taken shape—the German Concord Singers would participate; so would Otto Werner and Christy Hengel, musicians supreme; Miss New Ulm would be featured; a fire truck would carry the New Ulm High School hockey team, which had just won a regional tournament; there would be a few vans adorned with shamrocks; and Smiley Wiltscheck would ride on his three-wheel cycle while he played German polka music on his concertina.

The parade was billed as "St. Hermann's Parade on St. Patty's Day." And Brand is quick to point out that even William O'Connor managed to attend and graced a unit in the procession.

Sunshine broke through to warm the community residents who gathered at curbside to watch. The parade wound its way from Second South and Minnesota to the Glockenspiel near downtown New Ulm.

"I wore my yellow pants with my green jacket," Brand said. "We marched about six blocks. That's in deference to the Irish, who usually march in parades from one bar to another."

This year, Dempsey already is working busily, helping ensure that the parade will remain safely in Irish hands.

"The assignment of duties has gone out," he says.

"And we're sending out letters to lots of people in town. 'Even though you may have been disappointed last year,' we're writing, 'give it another chance.'"

Also instrumental in putting together this year's celebration will be O'Connor, Pat Kneefe and Father Harry Behan. Brand claims credit for putting Dempsey in touch with Father Behan, who was born in Ireland. "He's going to have to be grand marshal this year," Brand says. "I told Father Behan that."

Any such attempts to gain credit for helping New Ulm's Irish are likely to be ignored, however.

In fact, Dempsey says, claims by Brand that last year's St. Patrick's Day parade was the best ever are "obviously very partisan on his part."

Dempsey thinks he has the best word to describe last year's parade effort—"Minimal."

And, he adds, "It's not going to be tough to do better than they did last year."

Humor in the headlines

—First published on March 5, 1981

To see John Bremner, just think of Orson Welles when he was selling bottles of wine.

It's that sort of grandiose presence that this professor is able to bring into his classrooms at the University of Kansas. He's an imposing figure for students trying to absorb his demands for precision in speaking and in writing.

But Bremner also possesses a dandy sense of humor. He displayed that during a workshop conducted last year for editors of *The Free Press* and other Ottaway Newspapers. He also displayed his wonderful humor in a book he has written on the art of creating headlines.

In the book, entitled "HTK" (HTK is a code copy editors once wrote atop stories when they weren't sure, for one reason or another, what the headline would be. It meant "Hed to Kum."), Bremner takes a "how-not-to-do-it approach to the writing of news headlines."

As part of his teaching method, he presents headlines that should have been rejected somewhere on the copy desk.

Catholic Women Hear/Seeing Eye Dog Talk appeared in a newspaper in New Hampshire.

Avoid Having Baby/At the Dinner Table showed up in a Minneapolis newspaper.

And *Beauty Unveils Bust at Ceremony* made the news in San Diego.

Sometimes, Bremner writes, the problem revolves around being ambiguous:

Ike Says Nixon Can't Stand Pat, for example, from a newspaper in Georgia.

Broad to be Honored/As Man of the Year, from a newspaper in Los Angeles.

Or a favorite, *Many Antiques at DAR Meeting,* from another newspaper in California.

There also can be pronunciation problems, Bremner notes:

Actor Accidentally Shot in Debut, for example.

And headline writers who can't spell create all kinds of uncomfortable moments for family newspapers:

Actress Will Try/New Roll in Play
Girls Seek Births/On Track Team

Before taking our leave of Bremner, three more of his favorites deserve our attention:

Girl Becomes Methodist/After Delicate Operation
Man Pulls Needle From Foot/He Swallowed 66 Years Ago
Fatal Attack/Wasn't First/For Nasser.

Bremner taught us well

—First published on Aug. 6, 1987

John Bremner died last week.

Bremner taught journalism at the University of Kansas. Newspaper people who knew him considered Bremner one of this nation's foremost teachers of young reporters and copy editors. They recognized him as a charismatic professor, a tireless champion of good grammar, logic and rhetoric.

Bremner won our hearts here just a couple of years ago. During a conference in New York for copy editors, Bremner picked *The Free Press* as one of the three best-edited papers among 22 in the Ottaway newspaper organization.

A few jaws dropped in New York that day, for his selection meant that *Free Press* copy editors were performing as well as or better than our friends back East.

John Bremner knew his craft. He was a grammarian exemplar.

And he was forceful in passing along his knowledge. When he drove home a point in that booming voice of his, there was no question of his authority, of his command of the language. When it came to what was right and what was wrong about grammar, he didn't flinch. In short, if Bremner said you should use "who" rather than "whom," there was no debate.

Bremner died of cancer. He was 66.

He died at his home in Ponce Inlet, Fla., where he had lived since his retirement in 1985.

A native of Brisbane, Australia, Bremner had been ordained a Roman Catholic priest in 1943, and he had remained a priest for 24 years.

He was a fascinating personality.

The first time I met Bremner, someone commented that he looked a lot like Orson Welles.

It was obvious Bremner had been told this before.

He held his glass high in the middle of the room, and in that stentorian voice of his, he proclaimed, "I will serve no wine before its time."

Bremner came to the United States in 1950, earned a master's degree in journalism from Columbia University in New York City, and taught at the University of San Diego and the University of Iowa, where he received a doctorate in mass communications in 1965.

He came to the University of Kansas in 1969. He was the author of "HTK: A Study in News Headlines" in 1972, and "Words on Words: A Dictionary for Writers and Others Who Care About Words" in 1980.

We have those works in our library.

We will miss the man, and we will miss the personality.

But because of who he was and his enthusiasm about his craft, we will continue to learn from him.

Spring

o o o o o o o o o o o o o o o o o o o o o o o o o o o o o o o

For winter's rains and ruins are over,
And all the season of snows and sins;
The days dividing lover and lover,
The light that loses, the night that wins;
And time remembered is grief forgotten,
And frosts are slain and flowers begotten,
And in green underwood and cover
Blossom by blossom the spring begins.

—Algernon Charles Swinburne
"Atalanta in Calydon"

Sweet blissful Elysian

—First published on July 21, 1981

The ancient Greeks conceived of a realm where, after life, virtuous and happy souls might adjourn to pass eternity in a state of unblemished contentment. They called that place Elysium.

The word has an adjectival form: *Elysian—sweet blissful....*

A perfect place, it seems to me, to stop awhile, to take time to know the people, to see how they live, by what rules, to what purposes. And, after knowing them, to hear them speak about their lives. Then, by watching and listening, to test the truth of memory.

Those words help describe the nostalgic visions of C.W. Gusewelle, a columnist for the *Kansas City Star*, who has summered in Elysian, Minn., ever since he was a boy.

Gusewelle's love affair with Elysian began at the age of 4, when he first visited Lake Francis or Lake Frances—"a detail not yet locally agreed upon." There each year, he spent his summers with a favorite uncle.

"My earliest memories," he says, "are of arriving at night, of being carried into the cabin, of watching uncle try to start the fire with kerosene, of going down to the lake the next day, of walking through the foggy misty morning."

Gusewelle's writings on Elysian show his love for the community—and for the seasons he sees there.

"The northern morning comes with a rush on this, nearly the year's longest day," he writes.

"Birds chitter, and a black cat goes off quick-footed between the buildings. A truck motor whines out on the highway that bypasses the village. The street lights wink off together. Trees and the impending sunrise are reflected in the east window of the Odd Fellows Hall.

"In this slow fashion, it gets to be nearly 7 o'clock, and a man comes treading gingerly to try the door of Ralph's Corner Bar and find it locked. Other men come and rattle the handle and peer inside. And, in their great need, Ralph opens to them."

Gusewelle's articles on Elysian begin each spring.

"The idea," says Michael Waller, managing editor at the *Star,* "was that he would hit a small town in Minnesota and profile its citizens."

With Gusewelle already summering at the lake, it was logical that he focus on Elysian.

His reflections on seasons on the lake show Gusewelle's tremendous command of the language:

"In the spring of every year, when the sap rose, the Clarkes made maple syrup. After that, the boats and cabins had to be gotten ready for the season. Summer and fall, for the men, were the farming time. Then, toward Christmas, the ice was harvested from the lake—a thousand blocks of it, 18 inches square, to be sawed out and packed away under sawdust for the house and the cabins in the summer to follow.

"That was the rhythm of the year. The syrup, the cabins, the farming, the ice. There are other memories than work, of course: for Margaret, of snowy rides home from the village school, curled under horse blankets in the wagon-box sleigh; and, for Joe, of Sundays with his father on the lake.:

The history is precise, the writing is vivid, the characters are alive.

Gusewelle says he's not yet sure how his reflections will be viewed by the people of Elysian, the community "at the road's bend" with "454 inhabitants at the last count."

Most of them, he says, probably will never see the articles he writes for his Kansas City readers. In fact, he observes, he hasn't seen many of them in print himself.

Gusewelle shows great affection for the people he meets here:

"They never married," he writes. "Thus there is no immediate heir.

"'It kind of haunts you sometimes,' Joe Clarke says in his shy, soft voice. 'This farm has been in the Clarke name all that time. And one of these days it won't be.'

"Put to words, the notion smites them silent, Joe and Margaret both. They look at the table. In the coolness of the big house, a clock ticks.

"Then he speaks again, with something like a smile, and still softly—though it is still a cry wrenched from him.

"'You wouldn't really think,' he says, 'that anyone else would feel at ease here, would you?'

"And, in truth, you wouldn't."

Elysian certainly has changed during the nearly 44 years Gusewelle has been summering here.

"Now," he says, "some of the people I've loved most in the world are dead."

But the Elysian in Gusewelle's memory, and the people he has chosen to write about, have not changed much at all. And the people here could hardly ask for a biographer with more feeling for them or for their community.

"This part of the country, Minnesota, is central to what I am," Gusewelle says.

"I have loved the place a long time—and always as an outsider.

"It occurred to me that something someone cares so much about, someone should write about."

Spring brings hope

—First published on Feb. 9, 1982

Charles W. Gusewelle, who summers each year on Lake Elysian, has passed along an article he has written, a piece that so vividly describes the stirring of life as spring approaches.

"When the fist of winter closes again, as no doubt it will, consider offering your readers this small word of optimism," Gusewelle suggested to me.

He wrote this piece for the *Kansas City Star,* where he offers up three columns a week for his readers.

"Outside my window, a tree is budded," he writes.

"There is no explaining it. But neither is there any mistaking what meets the eye. The tree, a soft maple, has begun to reach in ancient faith toward a season that you and I cannot yet see.

"The punishment of ice and polar nights is fresh in mind. Both my cats remain disabled by the freeze. The cats, whose habit it is to crouch waiting for the door to come ajar, have given up trying to get out.

"They did get out once, a week or so ago, and came back sooner than they'd planned, ears laid flat, looks of astonishment on their faces. And they have taken instead to sprawling on the tops of steam radiators.

"It is the deep of February of a winter as fierce as any we have known.

"In the basement, the old furnace throbs and rumbles. An arctic wind whines at the window corners. Birds hunker on the branch and the squirrels have resorted to eating roof shingles.

"Brief autumn is forgotten. The turn to a gentler season is unimaginably remote. One foot set deliberately ahead of the next, like cattle plodding in blind file toward the comfort of a far-off barn, we march dutifully on but cannot notice the distance shortening at all.

"Daily it does shorten, though. And there, outside the window, is proof.

"There is nothing about winter that any of us can usefully tell a tree. The tree—this one, or the one from whose seed it grew, or the one that struck its root in colder earth than those—remembers them all.

"The hardest winters and the longest. The winters upon the edge of the vast, advancing ice; winters whose duration no calendar could measure. Winters that carved and forever changed the land. The memory of all that is written in the behavior of the descendant tree.

"What it tells is that spring always comes, or always has. Not necessarily soon. But sometime—always. Against that certainty, the tree prepares.

"Hence those out-of-season buds. A freezing rain has fallen overnight and, as I write this, ice sheathes every branch and twig. The buds are of a deep maroon color, and folded very tight, each the size of half a grain of popped corn. Unaffected by the cold, they wait their turn.

"In winter's agony, the bird remembers the stirring bug, the greening seed.

"The squirrel gnaws my bitter roof and imagines better fare.

"The cattle plod grayly on, and so do we.

"In all things alive, even in the hardest times, the tide of expectation is very patient, very strong."

The Music Man

—First published on March 25, 1987

Robert Preston left us with some very pleasant memories.

Even the most casual movie or Broadway show patron happily remembers Preston as the fast-talking "Professor" Harold Hill in "The Music Man."

But to many journalism students at the University of Minnesota, Preston left something more. His story was the centerpiece of the most interesting journalism class taught there—magazine writing, a course put together by Professor George S. Hage.

Hage knew Preston well, and he built his class around an article he had written about Preston for the *Saturday Evening Post.*

In the class, Hage traced the evolution of the article, from his first conception of the piece in the summer of 1958 to its publication on Dec. 6 of that year.

Hage met Preston during World War II while serving as an intelligence officer with the 555th Bombardment Squadron in Europe.

"There was considerable speculation as to whether this was the real Robert Preston," Hage remembers. Orders transferring Preston to the 555th had been cut using his real name, Robert P. Meservey, and Preston upon arriving didn't acknowledge his stage name.

"He was determined not to ride on his reputation as a film star," Hage said. "Bob didn't want that kind of service."

At the end of World War II, Preston was discharged and he returned to acting.

Hage remained to write a history of the Ninth Air Force, of which the 555th was just one part.

Later, while on rest-and-recuperation leave in Los Angeles—Hage said it seemed a little out of place "because I hadn't been in combat"—Hage contacted Preston and his wife, Catherine. He visited their home a few times during his stay there.

The idea for the *Post* article struck Hage in the summer of 1958, during his internship at the magazine.

"The Music Man" was enjoying a successful run on Broadway, and Hage decided to take in a matinee performance. Later he and his wife had dinner with the Prestons.

"It occurred to me afterwards that it would be a natural for a profile."

Hage discovered one problem, however. Preston already had turned down a request for an interview by another *Post* writer.

"He was quite jealous of his time because he was not trained as a singer, and he wanted to save his voice."

Preston agreed to let Hage do the article because with a writer who knew him "this would not require the investment of time that someone else would have to make."

In teaching students at the University, Hage detailed how he conducted his research, meeting with Preston and his wife a number of times and meeting with some of the Prestons' friends, and how he had to revise the article a number of times as *Post* editors read the piece and suggested changes.

On Dec. 6, 1958, Hage's piece appeared in the *Post*, under the title, "Happiest Actor on Broadway."

The *Post* featured the article as the lead teaser on the cover of that year's Christmas edition.

The Hages and the Prestons remained in touch over the years.

When Hage heard of Preston's death because of lung cancer, one of his first thoughts was to write a letter to Catherine.

"She was trained as a performer, too," Hage said. But as Hage had written in his *Post* article, her closest daily contact with the scene of her husband's success on Broadway was chauffeuring him to and from the Majestic Theater on West 44th Street.

"I feel that I can appreciate what she was going through," Hage said. "They had a very good marriage."

The Robert Preston article by Hage had remained in my memory ever since taking that three-credit class at Minnesota.

While visiting St. James, Minn., last year during the Christmas holidays, I spotted an old *Saturday Evening Post* in the window of Grandma's Emporium. The cover featured a Santa holding a wailing child, and in the upper right corner were the words, "Robert Preston of 'The Music Man.'"

Could this be the article featured in the magazine writing class, I asked myself. Sure enough, inside was the article with the byline, "By George Hage."

"Robert Preston," read the teaser on the first page of the article, "star of that smash hit, 'The Music Man,' can't sing and can't dance. Yet in a singing and dancing role, he proved that a movie star can triumph on the stage."

And, the people at the *Post* might add today, Robert Preston helped one of our favorite teachers triumph as well.

San Francisco beckons

—First published on April 17, 1987

If I've left my heart anywhere in San Francisco, it's with *Chronicle* columnist Herb Caen.

But please bear with me a moment before I raise Caen.

For me, San Francisco nostalgia begins with the Presidio, where I spent nearly a year in 1966 and 1967.

If you had to be in the Army, the Presidio was great duty, even if skipping a dress inspection one Saturday did cost me a promotion.

This opportunity to reminisce occurred last week when the American Society of Newspaper Editors (ASNE) held their annual convention at the world-class Fairmont Hotel.

Even the *Chronicle's* poor sister, *The San Francisco Examiner,* ran a piece on the Army installation: "Peaceful Presidio often under siege." Writer Dwight Chapin detailed this oldest continuously active military installation in the United States, describing it as "a city within a city, where 6,000 people work, 1,400 families and 600 soldiers live, and countless commuters drive through."

Then he called the base "one of the cushiest U.S. Army duty assignments in the world."

Well, the nerve! As a friend of mine once said, there were days when we didn't even get to the swimming pool until noon.

The *Examiner* writer quoted, among others, M. Gloria Heatherington, the editor who guided me during those Presidio days.

"I'm always happy to come to work," she told Chapin. "I live outside the main gate, and I walk, because it's so pretty. I see birds, butterflies, you name it. I think those of us who work here would like to see the Presidio remain just as it is—pristine and beautiful, almost the last vestige of sanity that's left in San Francisco."

Vestige of sanity is a good place to get back to Herb Caen.

Caen, who has written for newspapers for something over 50 years, writes a column six days a week for the *Chronicle.* He told his editors in San Francisco that he sometimes thinks he should just write seven days a week since on his day of rest he ends up worrying about "what I'm going to write about tomorrow anyway."

I hadn't read Caen regularly for 20 years. It didn't take long to remember what I had been missing.

Caen writes in a staccato style punctuated by ellipses. He calls it "three-dot journalism." If you live in or commute to San Francisco, he's the man you read to keep up with who's in, who's out and who has been seen where.

For example: "David Clark found one for the let's-try-that-again dept. in congressional candidate Kevin Wadsworth's campaign flyer: 'Think about Kevin Wadsworth because San Francisco deserves better!'"

Another: "The Rossmoor retirement community's recent fund-raiser to fight Alzheimer's disease was a party titled 'A Night to Remember.'...It's a special Easter season for J. Kenneth Little of Walnut Creek, who sent a bill to Medicare a few months ago and got this computerized reply: 'Your request is being denied because the services rendered occurred after the date of your death.' Ogawwwd. After the usual harrowing calls and correspondence, the computer admitted: 'Our records now show that you are alive.' Oh joy!"

And finally: "Stockbroker Phil Schaefer visited Sen. Ted Kennedy at his Palm Beach layout a few days ago, and, boggled in the poshness of it all, said, "Ted, I'm glad you know the difference between a just society and JUST society.' 'Right,' laughed Kennedy. 'Vote Democratic, live like a Republican.'"

In reading much of Caen, you almost have to be there. But when you finish his 40-inch piece every day, you really feel like you know what's happening in this man's city.

The powers that be among editors took it on the chin at their own convention. Some reporters were upset because while they were able to attend the ASNE sessions, they were not given lunch. Oh, they could buy $35 tickets so they could eat what the editors were getting for $20, but....

"So the editors are marking up each rubber chicken nearly 100 percent—to people in their own line of work," Steve Rubenstein wrote in the Examiner. "Is that nice? Is it ethical?"

"That's not all," he continued. "A secret document obtained by this columnist says the ASNE directors are getting a free $170 room at the Mark Hopkins Hotel in exchange for booking the convention." Michael Gartner, editor of the *Louisville Courier* and president of the society, passed the word along later that all directors were picking up their own tabs.

Caen spent very little time talking about the 661 editors who were invading his city.

"This may be the week you actually see some media celebs at the Wash. Sq. Barngrill, famous for same but not always delivering," he wrote. "Sam Donaldson lunches there Thurs., Peter Jennings dines there tomorrow night, and the place will be crawling all week with newspaper editors, in town for a nat'l convention."

Then Caen offered his cute response to this morsel of news: "Big deal!"

Those fascinating bats

—First published on June 18, 1981

Between the raindrops this past weekend, I crawled onto our roof to wrap thin wire mesh firmly over our chimney openings.

It's a ritual I perform every spring to keep the bats out.

In each of our homes, bats have flown through open doors, dropped in through chimneys or crawled down from attics to invade our living areas.

Over the years, bats have become an obsession with me. Their talents are fascinating. For example, if you can force your index finger into a hole up to your first knuckle, a bat can squeeze through. Also, while bats don't see well, their high-pitched squeaks while flying provide highly effective sonar navigation.

Minnesota's big brown bats are quite small compared to Southeast Asian fruit bats that boast wing spans of up to five feet or more. But even our smaller bats gobble up flying insects by the bushel.

The only problem occurs in June and July, when bats become extremely active because they're trying to mate. That means plenty of action not only for the bats but for those of us who occasionally host them in our homes.

My fascination with bats began on Van Brunt Street in 1970. A bat winged into our bedroom and wife Kay let out a life-ending midnight scream that immediately had me thinking, "Fire!"

It was the first time I'd ever seen a bat. I was terrified, but someone had to track down the prey. So while Kay "protected" our two sons in the oldest's bedroom, I fetched a broom and a hammer.

We had turned on the light in our bedroom, and the bat had sought out the darkness behind our dresser.

After swinging out the dresser, I trapped the bat in the straw end of the broom and used the hammer to nail him to the floor.

As I came out of the bedroom, suddenly a second bat swooped into the upstairs hallway. It eventually flew into a vacant room at the end of the hallway, and I slammed the door on it. The next day, I could not find it. It apparently had left the house through a tiny hole in a screen window.

When I brought the broom back to the kitchen closet, a third bat made its appearance. On the third or fourth swing with the broom handle, I managed to stun the bat and toss it outside.

Twice more in two years, bats found their way into our Van Brunt house.

One flew into our living room early one evening, leaving me splayed face down on the hardwood floor. Low-crawling to the front door, I managed to pull it open, and the bat cooperated by flying out.

On the second occasion, I discovered a bat dangling from a wooden cupboard in our rear entryway. I tried to hit it with a hammer, but missed. When it hissed at me, I cowered backward, nearly breaking a window pane with my backswing. Again I managed to open a door, and the bat flew out.

For me, these experiences were all traumatic.

But whenever I began feeling sorry for myself, I thought of a friend down the block. She had discovered one of the furry flyers in her cupboard—in a box of baking soda. The discovery put something of a damper on the baking she had been planning.

Three more confrontations have occurred since we left Van Brunt Street.

The first took place in a friend's Mankato home. He had spotted a bat at the bottom of his attic steps. In the heat of summer, the two of us bundled up in our winter best, to cover any skin areas the bat might attack. We armed ourselves with a tennis racket and hammer.

We opened the attic door, carefully, slowly.

Sure enough, there was the bat alongside a step.

I took the first swing, with my hammer. The animal's head fell off, and crumbled on the floor, like mud that had hardened and then been smashed into a thousand pieces. The bat must have been dead for several weeks.

The second confrontation took place in New Ulm, on State Street.

It probably was the most uneventful event in the series. By this time I had learned that a bat's sonar has a difficult time picking up the strings in a tennis racket, making it the most effective device to stun a bat. So one swing with the racket knocked the bat into our bedroom curtains. From there it was dumped outside.

The third confrontation took place in Red Wing. In many ways, it mirrored our first experience, though the midnight scream was not nearly as blood-curdling. On my knees near the bed, I grabbed a tennis racket that was being passed to me through a slit in our bedroom door. I watched the bat as it circled the room. My first swing didn't even come close as the bat fluttered easily over the racket. My second swing came closer, as I raised myself up to match the bat's trajectory, but again he lifted himself over my reach. On the third swing, I rose up, extending my arm completely, and hit the bat solidly, sending it senseless against the far wall. Bjorn Borg could not have done it better.

Through all the trauma, my admiration for bats has continued to grow.

I especially appreciate those insect diets they maintain.

But when June and July roll around, I grow a little nervous.

The bats must mate, I realize that. It's only natural. But each year, I hope one more time that they have the good taste to perform their acts outside.

Elvis is in the house

—First published on May 10, 1983

The expansive green lawn rises up gently to meet the walks surrounding the white colonial architecture of Graceland.

Stately trees shade the mansion where Elvis Presley lived for more than 20 years. It's early morning in Memphis; only two couples stroll on the grounds, walking along a lane that winds from one corner of the estate, where two guitar designs decorate two metal gates, to the rise of the hill where the mansion stands.

In this house on Aug. 16, 1977, Ginger Alden, the singer's latest girlfriend, awoke from a long day's sleep, walked into the bathroom adjoining the master bedroom of Graceland and found Presley lying dead on the bathroom floor.

Presley's death at age 42 sent shock waves through the rock 'n' roll generation. The county medical examiner in Memphis first ruled that Presley had died of natural causes.

But rumors, fed by a toxicology report showing traces of at least 10 prescription drugs in Presley's body, spawned stories that Presley had become a medication junkie who had fallen victim to his habit.

In testimony later, Presley's personal physician, Dr. George Nichopoulos, said:

- Presley routinely popped pills on tour before and after shows, and popped pills to go to sleep and to wake up. The doctor said Presley always took along three suitcases full of medical "supplies," including a large assortment of stimulants, depressants and painkillers—"so we wouldn't have to rely on an emergency room before a show."
- Presley probably was addicted to the painkiller Demerol and to barbiturates as well. Twice, first in October of 1973 and again in March of 1975, he was hospitalized and attempts were made to wean him from drugs, one time using methadone. But Presley was so distrustful of his doctors after learning that they were psychiatrists that he refused any further treatment.

"The life he lived, I suppose he had to stay hyped up," said a cab driver who was giving us his nickel-and-dime tour of Graceland on this morning. "I don't think he ever drank, though."

The cab driver, who said his name was Jackie Hungerfood, said Presley bought the home in about 1958. "They used to have big parties up there. He'd serve ice cream and Pepsi."

Presley often frequented the Hickory Log, a fast-food restaurant across the street, too, Hungerfood said. Or he'd have the food brought to him. "The Hickory Log, that's where he got his cheeseburgers. They used to send them over by the dozen."

Hungerfood said he first visited Graceland in 1961.

He wasn't a friend of the family, but "I did go to school with his girlfriend at South Side. He went to Humes High School. He was a year older than I was."

The numbers of people visiting Graceland have dwindled since the great crowds that swarmed in immediately following Presley's death.

Fans have continued to write on a stone wall that separates the estate from Elvis Presley Blvd., the street that brings visitors to Graceland. The words, "Elvis, even though you're gone..." or "Elvis, we still love you..." are erased from the wall from time to time, Hungerfood said, but his fans keep writing new verses.

Enough people still come in so the souvenir shops across the street from Graceland continue to do a thriving business.

Also, Hungerfood said, "They've opened a hotel here in Memphis and have named it after his hit record. They're calling it the 'Heartbreak Hotel.'" A pink Cadillac there has been converted into a salad bar.

One person has even tried to sell the vial Presley used to take his last drugs. The price tag—$1,000.

Presley's body has been moved out of Forest Hill Cemetery in Memphis. "Some clowns tried to dig up his body," Hungerfood said, "so they moved him up here."

His body now lies at Graceland alongside his father, Vernon, and his mother, Gladys.

Graceland's mansion houses a trophy room that features Presley's personal collection of gold records, awards and mementos; a collection of automobiles and other vehicles owned by Presley, including the famous pink Cadillac he bought for his mother early in his career; and a collection of show costumes valued at some $10,000 each.

The debate about Presley and the drugs continues.

"We're very sad over all this talk about Elvis, and it makes us feel very bad about the human race," Vester Presley, an uncle, told *People Magazine.*

Vester worked as a gatekeeper at Graceland for more than 20 years. He and Elvis's grandmother, Minnie Mae, 90, and his aunt, Delta Mae Briggs, remained in the mansion even after Presley's death.

They still find it upsetting when the talk of drugs dominates conversations about their most famous relative. As Vester told *People,* "Elvis was just a human being, just like everybody else."

Tammy's song

—First published on April 16, 1981

At birth, Tammy Erwin seemed destined to live a charmed life.

She was born on Christmas Day in 1957, and she was born in Washington, D.C., her nation's capital.

Her father, Benjamin, said his daughter "had just a normal childhood." She had no significant problems, he said, although there were times when his daughter got in with the wrong crowd. "Once in awhile," he observed, "kids do get into trouble."

But M.C. "Pete" and Norma Helquist of Mankato, Minn., whose son Jim married Tammy, said Tammy's problems as a child seemed to run deeper than her parents would admit.

When Tammy talked to the Helquists about her childhood, she talked of alcohol problems in her family, and she talked of being abused as a child. She talked of parents who had bad tempers, and she talked of parents who didn't really understand her.

"Tammy did bring out a lot of pity," Mrs. Helquist said. The only problem, Mrs. Helquist admitted, was that "we couldn't tell whether it was fact or fiction."

Tammy dropped out of high school after her sophomore year at Lee High School in Springfield, the Virginia community where she grew up and where her parents still live.

She had not done well in school. "She didn't apply herself, I felt," her father said.

The Helquists said they believe Tammy's basic intelligence was less than average, but they also believe that could have been caused by her use of drugs or alcohol.

Soon after John Helquist met Tammy in Springfield, Va., he brought her to meet his parents. They were married on March 28, 1976. They moved to Mankato and eventually had a son named Andy.

Not much time elapsed before the Helquists realized something was wrong with Tammy.

"She had great mood changes, and delusions," Mrs. Helquist said.

On one occasion, Jim came home and found Tammy sitting, talking to a garbage can. On another occasion, Tammy expressed a fear that Charles Manson was after her.

At times, Tammy would begin drinking, and she would end up at the detox center. Twice she called her family and threatened to kill herself. "She was definitely suicidal," Mrs. Helquist said.

"To say the least, she was a very mixed-up little girl."

In October of 1978, Tammy began her first stay at St. Peter State Hospital, committed by the Helquists.

Two months later, her father, her sister and her sister's husband came to St. Peter to visit her. Tammy left the state hospital and returned with them to Virginia.

"She wanted to come home," her father said, "so I brought her back up here.

"I wanted her to get back. She hadn't finished school."

The Helquists, not knowing where Tammy had gone, feared for her.

"We had a lot invested in Tammy," Helquist said, "because we were the only ones concerned. We were the only ones here who cared."

When St. Peter police discovered that Tammy was back in Virginia, the Helquists were able to relax again. "We were very much relieved," Helquist said, "because, at first, we didn't know where she was."

Tammy's problems persisted.

"When she got off the Valium," the medication she had been receiving in St. Peter, "she would get depressed," her father said. So Tammy agreed to a voluntary commitment at the Fairfax County Mental Hospital in Virginia.

"When she came out, she was good for two or three weeks," her father said. "Then she got mixed up with some of her old friends again."

As Tammy became more and more depressed, she wanted to return to her husband and her son in Mankato. So her father alerted the Helquists and put Tammy on a plane to the Twin Cities. Jim Helquist discovered Tammy had arrived when she called him from Bloomington. She had become confused and had boarded a bus after getting off the plane. "I thought I was in Mankato," she told her husband. He picked her up at a Bloomington police station.

On April 17, 1980, Tammy began her second stay at St. Peter State Hospital, committed by a judge.

By this time, Jim and Tammy realized their marriage was failing, and both realized they needed stronger mates.

"So they decided on a divorce," Mrs. Helquist said. "They thought that it would solve things. But they still couldn't stand to be apart."

The doctors at St. Peter weren't seeing much progress in Tammy. In a June 24 progress report, the "current diagnosis" was listed as schizophrenia. The report went on to explain that Tammy was "receiving anti-psychotic medications," but that she had not "responded positively....Involuntary treatment is necessary, as she is considered to be dangerous to herself due to neglect."

Even after discharge from the hospital, the report went on, "she will likely require structured and supervised conditions in her living situation."

Tammy remained at St. Peter several months. On Feb. 6, Tammy was reported as a walkaway from the state hospital. She had been wearing a white ski jacket and blue jeans. Authorities asked nearby residents to be on the lookout for a woman 5-foot-3, 105 pounds with light brown hair and blue eyes.

Two months later, on April 8, Tammy's body was discovered on the hospital grounds, by State Patrol officers in a helicopter checking traffic on Highway 169.

When Tammy had walked away from Community South on the hospital campus, it hadn't surprised the Helquists.

"When she became angry," Mrs. Helquist said, "she would often take a walk."

But on the night she walked away, temperatures dropped to 20 degrees below zero.

"It looked like she had gotten tired, sat down, and fell asleep," Mrs. Helquist said.

About 60 people attended a funeral service for Tammy at Bethel Baptist Church, 1001 N. Front St. Pastor Douglas Green, Pastor Jim Dinsmore and a number of Tammy's friends talked about her.

Tammy's mother, who is suffering from cancer, and her father weren't able to come from Virginia. "I sincerely regret my inability to be in attendance at Tammy's funeral," her father wrote. "It is a matter of both finance and my wife's disability. We will always remember Tammy for what she was."

The Helquists said they would remember Tammy fondly.

"She had the most beautiful smile," Mrs. Helquist said. "When she would smile, it was just like....And Tammy would be so lovable. You could put your arms around her, and love her, and she would just melt."

Those at Tammy's funeral sang, "Softly and Tenderly, Jesus is Calling."

The words of the song prompted one woman to say, "Many times, Tammy was calling, and we didn't always listen." She turned to the people in the church and said, "The next time, when someone calls, please listen."

Summer

o o o o o o o o o o o o o o o o o o o o o o o o o o o o o o

Shall I compare thee to a summer's day?
Thou art more lovely and more temperate;
Rough winds do shake the darling buds of May,
And summer's lease hath all too short a date;
Sometime too hot the eye of heaven shines,
And often is his gold complexion dimm'd;
And every fair from fair sometime declines,
By chance or nature's changing course untrimm'd;
But thy eternal summer shall not fade
Nor lose possession of that fair thou owest;
Nor shall Death brag thou wander'st in his shade,
When in eternal lines to time thou growest;
    So long as men can breathe or eyes can see,
    So long lives this and this gives life to thee.

—William Shakespeare
Eighteenth Sonnet

Grandparents

—First published on July 13, 1982

The two of us were about 10 years old when it happened.

We were playing cards with our grandfather, and when he left the table for a moment, I whispered to my cousin, "Let's set up the cards so we'll get all of the good ones."

Grandfather didn't see very well, and it's unlikely he would have noticed.

But grandmother, busy organizing some packages in her cupboards, did.

"You mustn't cheat on Grandpa," she said.

"Oh, we won't," we told her.

And with that quick promise to our grandmother, we never did.

The buildings that stood on our grandparents' farm south of St. James, Minn., are gone now.

The last time I walked there, just a couple of years ago, there was only an old corn crib and a solitary tree. I remember thinking, as the cold wind whipped the snow across the plowed fields, that it looked more like an Andrew Wyeth landscape than the farm where we grandchildren grew up.

Yet it was easy to recall the long gravel driveway that ran between the lilac bushes and the peonies, between the apple trees and the expansive lawn, the driveway that stretched to the large farm house.

There, under the biggest weeping willow tree most of us would see for 18 years, we learned from our grandparents.

In that back yard, much of it covered by gravel, grandfather posed for a photograph with his 2-year-old grandson—the two of us seated on a wagon behind a team of work horses.

As the years passed, those horses yielded to a tractor, but I could always say my roots reached back to the era of horse-drawn equipment.

On that farm, grandmother carried rusty water from a well near the barn, across the gravel backyard, and into the house.

She and grandfather carried corncobs, wood and coal from the summer kitchen into the house, fuel to stoke up the winter stove and warm—or at least try to warm—a house that leaked heat.

The farm held great treasures.

The red barn, stuffed with hay, harnesses and horses, served as our playground.

A haystack north of the barn featured a small indentation, a cave, a fort, at one end.

In a small storage shed near the barn, we found a stack of *Saturday Evening Posts,* enough magazines to keep us reading for many weeks.

In the house itself, grandmother and grandfather kept an upstairs room jammed with old harnesses, old furniture, old tools, wind-up record gramophones, thick wax records, and scores of old lamps, picture frames and other antiques.

There were piles of magazines there, too; old *Reader's Digests* we could read to make us sleepy when we stayed overnight.

Our country school was just down the road, less than a mile from the farm. So the farm served as a stopping-off place, a resting spot where we were likely to find freshly baked cookies or bread along with an afternoon greeting. Years later, when grandmother lived alone in town, her apartment offered the same kind of refuge.

On weekends, I would mow the farm's huge front lawn—and it was a huge lawn—and I would receive a dollar, sometimes a dollar and a quarter, for my efforts. That was big money for a little kid in those days.

What grandmother and grandfather tried to pass along endeared them to us.

Patience, for example. One year in school, my project was feeding pigs. Dad and I decided the best place to keep them was in the hog shed on grandmother and grandfather's farm. Patience prevailed, but barely, I suspect, especially on spring days when the west winds blew the odors from my pigs into their house.

And empathy. I can remember how aggressively we grandchildren played our games. Grandmother and grandfather watched us closely. "Mustn't be rough," was all grandmother would say, and it was enough to ensure that the youngest grandchildren wouldn't get hurt.

At grandfather's funeral in 1962, a great-uncle had come over to me. "He was a wonderful person," he said. "You're going to miss him very much."

A family friend said the same thing last Friday at grandmother's funeral. Grandmother had been in failing health for the past few years, but the friend appreciated the memories we held.

"What we all remember," she said, "is the grandma from just a few years ago. We're all going to miss her very much."

Flying with Lucky Lindy

—First published on July 21, 1983

"In 1923, a lanky, devil-may-care young pilot landed in Lou Fitcher's wheat field on the outskirts northwest of Madison Lake, Minn., and clambered out of his fabric-winged bi-plane with a big grin on his face."

That description of Charles Lindbergh's visit to Madison Lake appears in a booklet published this year by the Madison Lake Historical Society.

Agnes Borneke, 81, who still lives in Madison Lake, remembers standing in that wheat field, watching as Lindbergh climbed from the cockpit.

The barnstorming pilot asked, "Anybody want a ride?"

"That man," Mrs. Borneke smiles today. "All he had was five hours of solo experience—and we all dashed to ride with him."

As the Historical Society booklet says, Lindbergh landed in his "now-famous JN-4D 'Jenny,' a plane that he had cracked up all over Iowa corn fields but had patched up. [He] was still taking on riders—if they dared."

Mrs. Borneke at first did not join the rush to ride.

"I'll tell you one thing," she says. "Lindbergh was bashful—but I was so bashful."

It was Elmer Borneke, the man who would become her husband, who talked Mrs. Borneke into taking the flight.

Borneke already had ridden in the plane, and when he crawled out, he spotted her. "Little girl," he said, "you want a ride?" He paid the $5 for her.

Mrs. Borneke doesn't recall how the takeoff went, but she remembers the excitement of the 30-minute ride.

"I was scared, sure. There was nothing to hang onto."

Before taking off, Lindbergh had asked her future husband what the young lady would like to see on the flight. Borneke had pointed out his home, her home and some area lakes and a few Madison Lake landmarks.

Lindbergh told her that when he neared a landmark he would gesture downward, then bank the plane so she could see better. "When I do that," he told her, "that's something of interest to you."

"There were no seat belts. He turned that plane to the side, just like that, and I'd go down and grab onto whatever I could get ahold of.

"When I came back and landed and was bumping along, I was glad to be back."

As Bruce Larson, a Mankato State University history professor who has written about Lindbergh, said, "It turned out to be the only airplane ride of her life—whatever that may suggest."

"Not that I was afraid to fly again," Mrs. Borneke says.

She almost did fly again three or four years ago. She had planned to join a group for a trip to Hawaii. She became sick sometime before the departure, however, and was not able to go along.

The Historical Society published its booklet of history to commemorate Madison Lake's historical quilt.

Block 4 of that quilt depicts "Chas Lindbergh's Jenny Airplane."

Another portion of the booklet talks about Lindbergh's stay in Madison Lake.

"Glen Allyn, son of G.W. Allyn, hosted young Lindbergh—they were the same age—helped him service the plane and put him up in the 'City Hotel,' where he supposedly left grease on the doorknob on the No. 2 room in the southwest corner, grease the tale goes that the chambermaid would not wash off because it was left by Lindbergh."

The Bornekes followed Lindbergh's career with understandable interest.

Mrs. Borneke says her husband kept in occasional contact with Lindbergh. "I believe he called him 'Slim' or something like that.

"You take Lindbergh," she says today. "Maybe I was kind of silly, but I think he was one great man.

"For him to take off like that all by himself—all he had for company was a fly."

Canoe water-skiing

—First published on Sept. 1, 1981

Tommy Moore was slipping into his water skis Sunday when a bystander asked him if he was nervous.

"Not really," the 15-year-old skier said. "This is our second time, you know."

Moore moved into position along the dock at the Madison Lake cabin of his grandparents, and 11 oarsmen in Jack McGowan's homemade canoe strained to pull the craft away from the shore. They steered their craft in a tight circle and lined it up so Moore could grab the long nylon cord trailing the canoe.

"All set?" someone shouted from the canoe.

Moore, bobbing neck deep in the water, nodded, and the 11 people on board began paddling furiously, first as individuals, then quickly synchronizing by chanting "Stroke! Stroke! Stroke!" with each pull.

Almost immediately, Moore came up out of the water and began gliding over the surface on his two oversized water skis. People standing along the shore cheered, as they had on Aug. 23 when Moore first skied behind this canoe. And talk began again about submitting details of the feat for possible inclusion in the Guinness Book of World Records.

Tommy Moore's grandfather, Chuck Moore, 10 Saratoga St., Mankato, Minn., first thought of skiing behind McGowan's canoe.

"I asked him, 'I wonder if you could water-ski behind that thing?'" Moore remembers asking.

"He [McGowan, Route 1] said, 'I don't know, we'll have to try it sometime.'"

So on Aug. 23, the Moores attempted the feat just off-shore from their cottage on Madison Lake.

With grandson Tommy, son of Tom and Donna Moore, on the skis, three runs were made. And on each run, Tommy, also a good skier behind more conventional outboards, pulled himself out of the water and stayed up for about a minute.

The feat was duplicated on Sunday, and the paddlers said they were just as exhausted this time as they had been when they made history. As Keith Moore, one of the oarsmen, said, "I didn't know whether to yell 'Stroke! Stroke! Stroke!' or 'Heart Attack! Heart Attack! Heart Attack!'"

McGowan and his family built the canoe last winter when McGowan decided he wanted to put his entire 10-member clan into one boat.

Since then, crowds have gathered to get a glimpse of the 28-foot vessel: a French voyager-style canoe with upswept Viking prow and stern, appropriately decorated with green shamrocks.

"We didn't make it to look at, we made it to use," McGowan said earlier this year. "It's the kind of boat that, if it starts to fall apart, we can jump in and patch it right back."

Water skiing wasn't part of the plan when the canoe was built.

"We've seen no record of anyone who's paddled a canoe and pulled a water skier," Chuck Moore said. "We should have taken bets because a lot of people said, 'No way!'"

Added McGowan, "The funny thing is that this was hatched just over a couple cups of coffee. There wasn't even any beer involved."

When people hear that a water skier has been pulled by the canoe, Chuck Moore said, they tend to ask,

"'Well, how big a motor did you have on that?' But this was all manpower."

Tom Moore echoed that.

"I think we've found a great new way to save energy. OPEC can eat their hearts out."

A test for Norwegians

—First published on May 28, 1981

If you suspect there may be some Norwegian blood in your body, there's a 10-point quiz that has been designed especially for you.

I first ran across this quiz a couple of years ago in Red Wing, where it was being used as a test of readiness for induction into the Sons of Norway chapter there. I ran across it again this week while rummaging through a file of collectables—obviously, I had not buried it deep enough.

However, making the quiz public is only proper, in case some of you may be considering an application for membership in the Sons of Norway.

Following are the questions. The answers come later.

1) If you set your alarm at 8 in the evening for 9 in the morning, how much sleep will you get?

2) Does Great Britain have a fourth of July?

3) If some months have 30 days and some months have 31 days, how many months have 28 days?

4) If you carry a match into a dark room that has an oil lamp, an oil heater and a pile of kindling wood, which should you light first?

5) If your doctor gives you three pills and tells you to take one every half hour, how long will the pills last?

6) If you build a house with four sides, each with a southern exposure, and a bear wanders past, what color is the bear?

7) If you had 17 sheep and all but nine died, how many would you have left?

8) If you divide 30 by one-half and add 10, what do you have?

9) If there are three apples, and you take two from them, how many apples do you have?

10) How many species of each animal did Moses take with him on the ark?

You must answer 70 percent of the questions correctly to be admitted to the Sons of Norway, according to one official of the lodge I joined.

If you had trouble this time, just keep in mind that you should do better if you continue to practice.

The answers that follow should help you next time.

1) One hour (unless you have insomnia or unless, like me, your clock radio has p.m. and a.m. on the alarm display.

2) Every country that uses our type of calendar has a fourth of July.

3) Every month has at least 28 days.

4) The match.

5) One hour (You'd take one at zero minutes, the second at 30 minutes and the third at 60 minutes).

6) White. You would be living at the North Pole.

7) Nine.

8) 70.

9) You'd have the two you took.

10) Moses did not have an ark.

Another Black Friday

—First published on June 12, 1980

Tomorrow will be Friday the 13th, the only one threatening us this year.

This is the day when triskaidekaphobia and friggaphobia reign, and when hoards of people shun any significant activity: business wizards delay making deals, regular restaurant diners eat at home, shoppers avoid any sort of purchase, and people with their hearts set on marriage—or divorce—put their hopes on hold for a day.

Triskaidekaphobes fear the number 13. Friggaphobiacs fear Fridays.

The phobias have deep roots: Eve supposedly tempted Adam on a Friday, Noah's flood began on Friday, Solomon pushed the temple down on Friday, Christ was crucified on Friday.

"Operators of ocean liners hold ships until at least 12:01 a.m. Saturday following a Friday the 13th," one Associated Press correspondent discovered. "That's to calm the superstitious. It's not because the HMS Friday, whose construction was started on a Friday, set off on its maiden voyage on a Friday and was never heard from again."

In many buildings, architects leave out a 13th floor. Some airlines omit Seat No. 13 on their jets. House numbers in France skip from 12 to 14.

Certainly some good things have occurred on Friday the 13th.

Historians say Columbus first stepped onto North American soil on Friday, June 13, 1498. Francis Scott Key wrote The Star Spangled Banner on Friday, Sept. 13, 1814. Construction of the White House began on Friday, Oct. 13, 1792. (Although some political critics will argue that was not really a good thing.)

The newest method being used to cure phobias is forcing sufferers to experience their fears.

Persons with acrophobia, for example, are told to imagine themselves traveling to higher and higher floors of a building while remaining calm and relaxed. The imaginary trips are followed by actual expeditions to tall buildings or high bridges.

The theory is that persons with phobias develop avoidance behavior. Psychologists say that behavior, which has been reinforced over the years, must be broken if the patients are to be cured.

In "desensitization," patients are treated in groups or individually by being forced into phobic situations, less frightening ones at first, more threatening ones later on. This seems to weaken the avoidance behavior to the point where a person can tolerate the phobia.

Consider the desensitization patients will be forced to undergo for our most interesting phobias:

Agoraphobia—the fear of open places.

Ailurophobia—the fear of cats.

Androphobia—the fear of men.

Arachibutyrophobia—the fear of peanut butter sticking to the roof of your mouth.

Autophobia—the fear of being alone.

Clinophobia—the fear of beds.

Decidophobia—the fear of making decisions.

Ergophobia—the fear of work.

Gynophobia—the fear of women.

Ophidiophobia—the fear of snakes.

Peccatophobia—the fear of sinning.

Phobophobia—the fear of one's own fears.

If you fear Friday the 13th, a number of "cures" have been advocated over the years: leave your hat on in an elevator, wink at a white horse, whistle while passing a graveyard, avoid stirring coffee with your knife, refuse to open an umbrella indoors, or avoid picking up safety pins on the street.

One group in London, the Thirteen Club, at one time said poppycock to all those purported cures. "What's to be cured?" its members asked. The club hosted dinners at which 13 people were always present. Between courses, members would smash mirrors and spill salt.

That seemed to work for a time. But few people were surprised when members of the Thirteen Club announced that their luck had run out—they were "going out of business."

The cows party to polkas

—Updated from a feature published in August of 1970

Good Morning,
Good Morning,
It's Grand to be on Hand,
Good Morning,
Good Morning,
To You!

Roger Erickson and Maynard Speece begin their radio show every morning with that song.

Their dulcet, mellifluous voices set the tone for WCCO's Top of the Morning Show. And if the song is, at least occasionally, a little off-key, their audience doesn't mind.

I'm sitting in the WCCO Radio studio, reveling in this early morning tradition. I watch as they hold the final notes of their song, for dramatic effect, then throw on a good, old-time polka.

"Farmers have told us that they really like polkas," Erickson says. "They tell us that their milk cows produce better when we play polkas."

"Occasionally we will play a waltz," Speece chimes in. "I'll announced that we're playing it 'for all of you guys out there milking your three-quarter-teated Holstein.'"

That shows how close Erickson and Speece sometimes come to off-color humor. On occasion, it's gotten them into trouble.

Speece loves to tell how a train story once brought them a reprimand.

"Roger," Speece asked on the air, "do you know why it takes the train so long to get from Princeton to Milaca?"

"No, Maynard, why does it take the train so long to get from Princeton to Milaca?"

"Because it stops at Long Siding and Pease."

"Early morning is the best time to do radio," Erickson says. "In the early morning, you can get away with more."

Usually, he might have added. The "Long Siding and Pease" exchange drew them a caution from WCCO's general manager. Nonetheless, most listeners certainly would say, Erickson and Speece usually stay well within the boundaries of good taste.

Erickson starts earliest, at 5 p.m. He provides weather reports, traffic updates and, if blizzards force school closings, Erickson will read them all—it's a radio service that he has turned into an art form.

Speece joins in at 6:05 a.m. They salute four or five communities around the Upper Midwest, shouting, "Hello, Long Siding," "Hello, Pease," or whatever, and then they launch into their Good Morning song.

With both on board, the program really gets rolling, with lively music, corny jokes, and plenty of wit. Both show quick humor.

When Paul Giel, the sports director walks into the booth, I stand up to shake his hand and say, "I have always wanted to meet a great athlete."

"Well, don't worry about that," Erickson says, "meet Paul anyway." Giel, a standout college athlete at the University of Minnesota in both football and baseball and a Major League baseball pitcher, just laughs at Erickson. He knows what to expect from these two.

When they begin giving an update on a longshoreman's strike in San Francisco, Erickson says, "Yes, it's a dock strike." Speece chimes in, "I think that's a paradox. I think there are two docks on strike."

■

Erickson, who grew up on a farm near Winthrop, came to the University of Minnesota to study speech and theater. He came to WCCO Radio in 1959. He first served as an announcer and also appeared as Bozo the Clown on WCCO-TV. After years of getting up at 4 a.m. ("I like that time because I don't have to battle any traffic to get to work," he would say.), he retired in 1998.

"It's been a great run," Erickson said when he stepped aside after 38 years at WCCO. "How lucky can you be?"

Speece grew up on a farm near Meadowlands, a small farming community about 40 miles northwest of Duluth. He also attended the University of Minnesota, in the College of Agriculture. He joined WCCO Radio as farm service director in August of 1952, and he worked there 25 years.

■

Considering their sharp sense of humor, it's not surprising they lasted so long. Still, maybe Erickson was right—Speece could get away with more early in the morning.

As well as at his retirement party in 1978, when he told stories such as this:

"I was in this hotel one night," Speece said to his audience, "and there was a knock at the door. I got up, opened the door and there was a beautiful gal. She took one look at me and said, 'Oh—my G—! I must have the wrong room.' I said, 'Oh, no! You have the right room, but you are 30 years too late.'"

Maynard Speece returns

—First published on Oct. 22, 1981

Just when you thought it was safe to go back into the water....
—An advertisement for Jaws II

Just when you thought you might never have to "endure" another joke from Maynard Speece, Speece's wife, Marigold, has written a book.

Maynard, it's called, *Humor through the years with Maynard Speece.*

The book features some of the classics Speece made famous as a broadcaster with WCCO Radio and as a banquet speaker throughout the country.

For years, Speece had planned to write his own book of humor. In anticipation of that four or five years ago, he dictated a number of his favorites to Marigold.

But in June of 1978, just four months after he retired as farm director of WCCO Radio, Speece suffered a stroke. The stroke left him with aphasia, a speech disability, and it paralyzed his right side. Speece is only now beginning to speak again, and he is learning to write with his left hand.

Maynard the book came out just this month, and the collection helps Speece realize that longtime ambition to see his "works" in print.

"My folks were poor," Maynard says in the collection. "There were seven of us in the family, five boys and two girls, and I was one of the boys. Times were so hard, my Mother used to put me and my older brother in the same diaper—just to make ends meet."

"I was sitting in the porch swing with my girl one night when her father leaned his head out of the window of the upstairs bedroom and said, 'Young man, we turn the lights out around here at 10 o'clock." I said, 'Well, that's OK, sir, we have no intentions of reading.'"

"I think there are some advantages to being born and raised on a farm. You reach a point where you can understand the animals. One day I was down by the pig pen. One old sow said to the other, 'Have you heard from your boar friend lately?' And the other old sow said, 'Yes, I had a litter from him yesterday.'"

Maynard and Marigold Speece were in Mankato Monday, visiting Maynard's sister and brother-in-law, Garnet and Mervin Nelson, 106 Timberlane.

Maynard and Mervin were playing pinochle, and Maynard claimed he had won two of three games and was leading in the fourth.

Through therapy and exercise, Speece has learned to walk again, using only a cane for balance. He exercises by swimming at Courage Center. He is working with a speech pathologist, too. He is unable to initiate conversation, Marigold said, but "if given a clue," he can find the right word to finish a sentence. He comprehends comments from others, and, best of all, he still appreciates humor, reveling in it with his hearty laugh.

In the book, Marigold writes that Maynard continues to personify what has been his philosophy over the years: "Some people endure life," Speece once said. "I enjoy it."

"I have a friend who is a gynecologist, and has a very jealous wife," Speece dictated. "He told me the other day that he had had a very bad day. At the end of this difficult day, his last patient was a friend of the family. He said, 'Myrtle, I've had a rough day. Do you mind if we have a cup of coffee before I examine you?' She said, 'No, I'm in no hurry—take a break.' While they were having their coffee, the doctor noticed the silhouette of his jealous wife through the frosted glass door of his office. In near panic, he said, 'Here comes my jealous wife. Hurry up—take off your clothes and get up on that table.'"

"Then there was the psychiatrist who said to the tearful woman, 'You must cheer up. Be happy.' 'How can I be happy? Twelve children I've had with that husband of mine, and he doesn't love me. What have I got to be happy with?' 'Well,' said the doctor, 'imagine if he did love you.'"

"A proud father phoned the newspaper and reported the birth of twin girls. The person at the news desk didn't quite get the message and said, 'Will you repeat that?' The father replied, 'Not if I can help it.'"

In addition to the humor, the book also includes 14 drawings, some 100 photographs, and considerable biographical material from Speece's 25 years as farm director at WCCO.

"The secret to success in using humor is knowing what to use and what not to use, and then crowd it as close to the line as you can get," Speece once told a *Minneapolis Star* reporter. "You're walking a tightrope and there are many who have tried it and gotten into trouble."

In the book, Marigold tells of her husband and Roger Erickson, his partner on WCCO's Top of the Morning Show, almost getting into trouble.

"Roger," Speece asked, "do you know why it takes the train so long to get from Princeton to Milaca?"

"No, Maynard, why does it take the train so long to get from Princeton to Milaca?"

"Because it stops at Long Siding and Pease."

WCCO's general manager at the time called both announcers in after that exchange. "The story about Long Siding and Pease?" he said. "We go for informality, but this is ridiculous."

The following morning, in their salutes to towns, which always preceded the "Good Morning" song, the announcers saluted both Long Siding and Pease. Said Speece, "It was like kicking a tin can along the sidewalk."

Outhouse theories reign

—First published on Aug. 11, 1981

Shelley Cords of Box 584, Lake Crystal, Minn., calls herself an "avid outhouse enthusiast."

"I happen to be the proud owner of a custom-built outhouse, complete with a quarter moon in the door," she writes.

"It was given to me to commemorate my college graduation. What else do you give someone receiving their B.S. degree in parks and recreation?"

Like many of us, Cords hasn't discovered definitively why that quarter moon graced most outhouses (and graces those still in use).

However, Cords has spent some time considering the matter, and she offers three theories on the origin of the quarter moon.

"Astrological theory—Speculations that certain astrological cycles/phenomena affect human life as well as the animal kingdom (like when the fish are bitin') may have resulted in quarter moons as a sign of good luck—you know, the natural 'forces' worked best under these conditions (relief from constipation, for instance)—or quarter moons may have been used to ward off superstitions (Full moons bring out werewolves).

"Mooning theory—During the Victorian Era, the genteel life brought out the modesty in people. Women were covered from head to foot, and a concern for privacy was practically written law.

"Getting relief in the wide-open spaces would more properly signify a 'full moon.' But being confined securely behind an outhouse door more closely signifies the 'quarter moon,' since, after all, the privy was still outdoors.

"Instinct may have told the nostalgic Victorians that the once-favored wide open spaces was not all bad (the aroma being a major factor), and the constant reminder of a quarter moon shadow cast onto the interior wall might have made them feel they were still squatting outside.

"**The moon and star theory**—In the book, *Privy*, by Janet and Richard Strombeck, it says, 'We have been told the moon meant it was for ladies and a star would be for gents. That way, anyone could stay out of trouble, even if unable to read.'

"My conclusion on that: We see more quarter moons, probably because the ladies used them more, since men usually water the trees anyway."

To me, the final theory sounds the most feasible.

You had to let light into those little boxes somehow. And to be able to fulfill that necessity and at the same time identify the men's room and the women's room displays good American ingenuity.

Cords confirms that thought: "Apparently," she writes, "American privies were the only ones to have moons or stars."

Outhouse theories II

—First published on Aug. 27, 1981

Margaret Whitlock of 10 Roblen Court offers further evidence that crescent moons cut into outhouses meant "ladies only."

In *Our Vanishing Landscape* by Eric Sloane, we read about the early American outhouse.

"Wall-papered and curtained, discreetly embowered at a considerable distance from the back of the house, was the privy. It was not regarded with the petty humor that surrounds it today. The familiar crescent cut into these doors originally designated the building as being one reserved for ladies, for the moon was always regarded as being female. The sun being regarded as male, it was once used as the design on the doors for gentlemen."

Thus, *Our Vanishing Landscape,* which Mrs. Whitlock ran across at the Orchard Road Paperback Exchange, 1010 Orchard Road, at least in part supports the "moon and star theory" advanced here Aug. 11 by Shelley Cords of Lake Crystal.

In another passage, Sloane writes:

"It stretches the modern imagination to think of a privy being architecturally exquisite, yet those built on the southern plantations were delicately designed, often surrounded by statuary, and always in strict keeping with the style of the main house. It is a far cry from the back-house shed that New England boys overturned as Hollowe'en sport, to the Greek Revival privies of the early South. In many cases where the plantation house was large and rambling, the builder found his fullest expression concentrated in this one small outbuilding, and the privy became a better piece of architecture than the home itself."

A couple of readers had asked where they could obtain a copy of *Muddled Meanderings in an Outhouse,* the volume that precipitated these gentle passages about outhouses.

Larry Norland, 716 Lake St., passes along a copy of *Muddled Meanderings,* Number 2, which he picked up in the Black Hills.

"The sole purpose of my purchasing the enclosed book," he writes, "was to bring back proof or reasons to explain the crescents found on outhouses and hopefully to lay to rest the reasons or need to have further outhouse columns."

The author of the book is Bob Ross. The book costs $2.95, and copies are available from Ross at P.O. Box 927, Bozeman, Mont. 59715.

Norland said he plans to read the book when it's returned to him.

"As one who has grown up on a farm in Iowa in the '40s and '50s, I have memories (fond?) of an outhouse that I knew as an intimate friend. The one thing I disliked about it was the northwest winds in sub-zero weather."

Norland urged a recitation of "Lunar Mythology," one of the offerings in Ross's book.

It, too, provides some support for the "moon and star theory":

Many and many a year ago—about 400 years B.C.
The Romans gazed at the moon above with a strange mythology.
They believed the moon was a goddess—a virgin maiden fair.
They named the goddess Diana and put a crescent moon in her hair.
The crescent became a symbol that stands for women kind.
And so the symbol was handed down to the outhouse out behind.
The privy that has the quarter moon carved in the door or side.
Signifies that the fairer sex should only be inside.
It seems the men had a symbol, too, to keep on even par.
It represented Sol, the sun, with a circle or a star.
Throughout the many years of use the sun symbol fell by the way.
But the crescent moon still prevails to be used by all today.

Sven and Ole are back

—First published on Nov. 10, 1981

With all the Scandinavians in Southern Minnesota, it's not surprising that Sven and Ole jokes continue to thrive.

Several weekly newspapers serving this area find they can hardly keep apace of the demand for Scandinavian humor.

Ken Anderson of the *Cottonwood County Citizen* tucks a Sven and Ole offering into his column a couple of times each week.

A couple of his most recent efforts:

■ Big Ole was driving down the highway when he was pulled over by a policeman. The officer walked over to Ole's pickup and said, "I'm afraid your wife fell out of the back of your camper a couple of miles back."

"T'ank goodness," exclaimed Ole. "Ay t'ought Ay had gone deaf."

■ Big Ole was walking down the street one dark night when two thugs jumped him. Although Big Ole put up a terrific fight, the two men finally got the best of him.

After they finished their search, the thugs were amazed at the small amount of money they found in Ole's pockets.

"You mean you put up a fight like that for just 67 cents?" one of the thugs asked.

"Shucks, no," Ole said. "I thought you were after the $500 in my shoe."

At the *Lafayette-Nicollet Ledger,* Deborah L. Hanson does the honors:

■ Two Swedes were discussing married life.

"I never knew vat real happiness vas until I got married," said the first one.

"Ya, I know vat you mean," said the other one, "but by den it's too late."

■ A Norwegian was building a fence and working with great speed. When asked why he was in such a hurry, he said, "I'm trying to get done before I run outta nails."

■ Mrs. Elvendahl mailed a package to her son with a note reading: "Magnus, I'm sending your vest. To save weight, I've cut off all the buttons. Your loving mother.

"P.S.—They're in the top pocket."

R. A. Gilbertson at the *Wells Mirror* devotes entire columns to such "humor."

■ Lars: Say, Ole, I went by your house last night and noticed you kissing your wife in the window.

Ole: The yoke's on you, Lars. I wasn't even home last night.

■ A Norwegian and a Swede were in a bar, watching the evening 10 o'clock news on the TV. This fellow was on the ledge of a high building, threatening to jump to his death. The Norwegian said, "I'll bet you 10 bucks that he jumps." The Swede said, "I'll be you 10 bucks that he doesn't." The fellow on the ledge jumped to his death. The Norwegian picked up his money, but, feeling guilty about it, he said, "I saw him jump on the 6 o'clock news." The Swede said, "So did I, but I didn't think he'd be dumb enough to do it again."

The latest story making the rounds comes from Anderson:

Big Ole was selected to sit on a jury. One of the first cases to be heard concerned a man who was accused of lewd and lascivious behavior. The victim of the alleged transgression, a sedate lady, was called upon to testify. Because of the delicate nature of the matter being considered, she was allowed to write what the defendant had said rather that repeat it out loud.

As the note was passed to the jurors, the pretty young panelist seated next to Ole noticed he had fallen sound asleep. She gave him a shot in the ribs, and Ole awoke with a start. She passed him the note, and the bleary eyed Ole opened it up to read.

A big smile creased Ole's face as he finished the message. He nodded to the sweet young thing next to him and tucked the note into his pocket.

Holy Cow, it's Harry!

—First published on Feb. 22, 1998

Harry Caray was a friend of mine.

OK, he didn't know me from any other baseball fan. But many of us who listened to Caray broadcast baseball games over the years thought of him as a friend.

Caray, who had been the voice of the Chicago Cubs for 15 years, died Wednesday, four days after collapsing at a Valentine's Day dinner at a restaurant in Rancho Mirage, Calif.

Harry Caray's voice first came my way when he announced games for the St. Louis Cardinals. Under the cover of darkness, the air waves from KMOX Radio in St. Louis reached our farm in Southern Minnesota. I can remember sneaking the radio under the covers late at night and listening to Caray, and I can remember being ever fearful that some exciting play would send him into a paroxysm of ecstasy and one of my parents would hear him screaming.

During 1971, Caray moved to the Chicago market, having been booted by the Busch family in St. Louis. He would broadcast first for the White Sox and then for the Cubs. My little family moved to Chicago, too, and we lived in the northwest suburbs for three years. Never during those three years did I make it to watch either the White Sox or the Cubs. Later, back in Minnesota, I vowed to return to Chicago often and to make Wrigley Field an essential part of each visit.

By the time I finally did get to Wrigley, Caray had become a fixture for the Cubs. Watching baseball in Wrigley Field was heaven for a baseball fan, enjoying that natural grass, appreciating the ivy vines growing on the outfield walls and being able to sit either in those distant sun-soaked bleachers or close behind the dugouts, so close to the field that you always ran the risk of being drilled with a foul line drive.

Caray played an important part in the annual ritual.

Being able to sit at Wrigley and watch and listen as Caray led the crowd in singing "Take Me Out to the Ballgame" entering the bottom of the seventh inning was baseball at its best.

Sportswriters sitting in the press box could enjoy Caray even while watching the game. Being able to hear Caray's voice in the next booth and even to watch as he endured the clouds of smoke from fellow announcer Steve Stone's ever-present cigar always added great flavor to the experience.

During his last few years, Caray began to mangle multisyllabic names, even more than he did during his early years, and even ended up with players in the game who already had been replaced. Stone, to his credit, often tried to save him, but for Caray's fans, it only endeared him to us even more.

The players never grew weary of Caray. Even the great ones loved him—you could see it on their faces as they greeted him. When Barry Bonds, the San Francisco Giants great, and his father, Bobby, came to town, they would make a beeline for Caray. Bonds' ego would show with other announcers. For example, he spoke with Wayne Laravee, another Cubs announcer who also called the Chicago Bulls games, about how he would be able to whip Michael Jordan in a game of one-on-one. Bonds would never perform that routine for Caray. In fact, Caray, eavesdropping on Bonds and Laravee, just smiled and shook his head. Even Caray knew the younger Bonds probably wouldn't score a single point, unless Jordan gave him a free pass.

Three experiences with Caray stand out for me.

On my last visit to Wrigley Field, he held out his hand near the batting cage and said, "Hey, great to see you, buddy." I know he had no idea he had seen me before; he was just being Harry Caray.

A year earlier, I had brought a baseball to Caray to sign. His production manager had told me she would ask him. But when I saw her distracted, I barged right in on Caray. "Hey, you could have brought this to me earlier," he said, obviously peeved because I had caused him to stop writing out the lineups. But he signed the baseball with his trademark "Holy Cow" and wrote "Harry Caray" right below it. Then he handed the baseball back to me with a friendly, "OK, here you go, buddy."

The year before, I had dined at Harry Caray's restaurant with the editor of *Bleacher Banter,* a publication designed for Chicago Cubs fans. At the restaurant, I always ordered a steak and a Budweiser because Caray was a spokesman for Bud. We were sitting there when, suddenly, Caray came walking in with his wife on his arm, and with another couple in tow. They sat down at Caray's usual table in a corner of the restaurant. A few moments later, Mark Grace, then the Cubs first-baseman, came in and sat down with a young lady. My dining partner ended up spending most of her time bantering with Caray at his table and Grace at his.

She also sent a round of drinks to the Caray table and a round of drinks to the Grace table. I ended up picking up the tab.

I will continue to visit Wrigley Field and Harry Caray's restaurant. It won't ever be quite the same without him, but it will be nostalgic for me.

It's satisfying to think that Caray might now be announcing games for "Shoeless" Joe Jackson and his friends playing on the "Field of Dreams." I've heard people talk about leaving this world and, as they're slipping away, seeing someone bathed in bright light, holding out a hand and calling them home. For most of us, that person will be a mother or a father. For me, I wouldn't mind at all if they brought along Harry.

Buffalo Bill rides again

—First published on Aug. 26, 1980

When the Pony Express began in 1860, 15-year-old Bill Cody was one of the first riders to sign up.

Years later, he would boast about galloping into Three Crossings, his home station, and discovering "that the rider who was expected to take the trip out...had been killed, and...there was no one to fill his place.

"I did not hesitate for a moment to undertake an extra ride of 85 miles to Rocky Ridge, and I arrived...on time. I then turned back and rode to Red Buttes, my starting place,...a distance of 322 miles."

Buffalo Bill Cody never did spare words in building his own legend, or that of the Pony Express. Don Russell, one of his biographers, wrote: "For three decades, a representation of the Pony Express was a spectacle at every performance of Buffalo Bill's Wild West. No other act was more consistently on its program...."

That Wild West show came to St. James 72 years ago today, and Buffalo Bill Cody came with it. It was a day Herb Stolze will never forget.

On Aug. 26, 1908, Stolze was 12 years old.

Stolze and his father had driven to the train depot in the family buggy, to watch the Wild West show performers as they came into town and unloaded their equipment.

Stolze spotted Buffalo Bill Cody standing near a team of two white horses. The matching horses were hitched to Cody's chauffeur-driven carriage, "a carriage like you'd see in England," Stolze says.

"He was a tall man, a good 6 feet, and he wore a mustache.

"He was running his hands over the horses. He was wearing white gloves, and he was checking for dust.

"I saw him pet the horse, and then he looked in the palm of his hand. 'Perfect,' he said.

"About the time he was going to get into his coach, he saw me. 'How are ya doin', son?' he said.

"'Fine,' I said. 'We just came down to see ya.'

"That's when I shook hands with him. My dad had his team hitched to his buggy, and he said, 'Let's follow Buffalo Bill out to the fairgrounds.'"

The Wild West show was being set up on the south end of the fairgrounds.

Stolze remembers being nearly overwhelmed as he drank in that scene.

Community residents swarmed over the fairground site. "You couldn't number them," Stolze said. "The town was full. The town was packed with people.

"I say to this day, the fairgrounds will never see a crowd like turned out to see Buffalo Bill that day."

In an interview with the *St. James Plaindealer* last year, Stolze told of the hundreds of Indians, cowboys, buffalo and horses Buffalo Bill's performers brought into town for the spectacle.

The show was to feature a depiction of the Battle of Summit Springs, with many Indians and government forces battling. There was to be "a savage display of frightful warfare," and "a great train holdup featuring bandit hunters of the Union Pacific." And there were to be Russian Cossacks, Irish lancers, South American gauchos, U.S. rough riders and American cowboys, all performing daring deeds of riding.

Buffalo Bill had planned two performances at St. James. But neither performance went on.

As the Aug. 29, 1908, *Plaindealer* reported, "Buffalo Bill's Wild West show arrived in the city on Wednesday morning, but the rain had made the ground so soft that it was found impossible to move the equipage to the fairgrounds, where the performance was to have been held.

"After hauling a few heavy vans to the grounds, the attempt was given up. A good many people came to town, but about all they saw was the mud-bedraggled circus hands and horses pulling the wagons through the streets."

It had rained almost steadily for about a week, Stolze recalls.

When wagons for the show rolled into the fairgrounds, "they had to put three teams of horses on each wagon, and they had an elephant on each wheel, lifting on the hub, and one elephant behind, pushing with his head."

When Buffalo Bill saw the quagmire, he said, "Load up, men, we're going to be too late for even one show. We'll never get anything put together in time to show one show."

So Stolze, now 84, missed his chance to see the Wild West show and to steal a glimpse of those Pony Express days. Yet meeting Bill Cody and the spur-of-the-moment handshake meant plenty.

"This Buffalo Bill," Stolze said, "I'll never forget this."

Autumn

o o o o o o o o o o o o o o o o o o o o o o o o o o o o o

O wild West Wind, thou breath of Autumn's being,
Thou, from whose unseen presence the leaves dead
Are driven, like ghosts from an enchanter fleeing,

Yellow, and black, and pale, and hectic red,
Pestilence-stricken multitudes: O thou,
Who chariotest to their dark wintry bed

The winged seeds, where they lie cold and low,
Each like a corpse within its grave, until
Thine azure sister of the Spring shall blow

Her clarion o'er the dreaming earth, and fill
(Driving sweet buds like flocks to feed in air)
With living hues and odors plain and hill:

Wild Spirit, which art moving everywhere;
Destroyer and preserver; hear, oh, hear!

—Percy Bysshe Shelley
"Ode to the West Wind"

Caring for a daughter

—First published on Sept. 9, 1982

We had spent much of the morning in Edward Bjorkman's alfalfa field, broiling under the hot sun, piling bales onto his hay rack.

I can remember the heat. I can remember our sweat. And I can remember Clara Bjorkman walking across the road with a large basket crammed with sandwiches, cookies, cakes, apples, coffee and Kool-Aid, a lunch that would require a good half hour to finish.

The Bjorkmans operated a small farm about six miles south of St. James, Minn.

The two of them were a typical farm couple running a typical homestead.

But they possessed something special. Much of the Bjorkmans' lives revolved around their daughter, a spindly girl who rested in a wheelchair inside their white farm home; and in their unwavering devotion to her, they seemed to find a powerful strength.

Bernice Bjorkman had just reached her 23rd year when multiple sclerosis struck her down.

She had graduated from St. James High School in 1945 and from Mankato Teachers College in 1949. She had taught about a year and a half in the Morgan school district when the disease hit.

The Bjorkmans sought help from doctors and clinics throughout the United States.

They implemented a regimen of therapy in their home. An exercise bicycle and parallel bars Bernice could walk between to strengthen her body stood in her bedroom.

But for most of her last 26 years, Bernice would be confined to her wheelchair.

When our family visited the Bjorkmans, the scene was always similar—Bernice would be seated in the living room, religious books stacked on tables surrounding her, a blanket covering her legs, and her knitting needles always close at hand.

As long as Bernice could, she continued to knit, remembers LaVern Pearson, a nephew of the Bjorkmans, who today farms just half a mile from where the Bjorkmans lived.

Bernice would knit afghans as well as squares used to make blankets for veterans homes.

Visiting the Bjorkmans always meant good food. The smell of baking or canning usually filled the house. Visitors would receive cookies or doughnuts. Clara often would make Jell-O with oranges in it, Pearson said—"That's the thing I remember."

Pearson served as conservator for Clara and Bernice after their husband and father died. "I think we were the closest to them of anyone," he said.

He was able to see as well as anyone how well Clara bore up under the burden of having her only child struck down, never able to walk again.

"Clara always wanted to give," Pearson said. On various occasions, she sent money to help Korean children.

"When we'd come to visit, she'd say, 'You go home, you have enough work to do at home.'"

Clara would show her concern, too, with her last words as visitors walked out the door. "Drive careful," she would say.

After Edward died of a heart attack, Clara and Bernice stayed in their home for two more winters. But even with a housekeeper to help them, "it was too hard to stay on the farm," Pearson said. The family decided to move Bernice to Luther Memorial Home in Madelia.

Clara moved off the farm, too, and took up residence in a Madelia house.

Just three months later, on Dec. 28, 1967, Clara also moved into the nursing home.

For the next nine years, Clara helped workers at the home care for her daughter.

"Bernice was always cheerful," Pearson said. "She'd always laugh when you told her a joke." That held true even near the end of her life, when her speech had deteriorated to the point where she could hardly be understood.

Late in 1976, both mother and daughter were admitted to Madelia Community Hospital.

Clara was 78, Bernice was 49. Clara had been suffering from a great deal of internal bleeding, and she received five units of blood at the hospital. Only Clara's determination to continue caring for her daughter kept her alive, family friends were saying.

"Even when she knew she was dying," Pearson said, "she told us we should be going home. She was worried that we should be taking care of our business."

The day before they died that October, Clara and Bernice were brought into the same room. They were able to touch one another, and Pearson believes that Clara knew what was happening.

Pearson was with both of them when they died, Bernice first at 3:35 a.m., then Clara at 10:10 p.m., both on Oct. 3.

"I went and told Clara that Bernice had died," Pearson recalled. "It sounded like she said, 'That's nice.'

"The peace she got when she heard Bernice had died—she just relaxed and was at peace."

It was appropriate that Oct. 3 was a Sunday, too, Pearson said.

"What kept Clara going was her faith," he said. "She always felt God was in control of the situation.

"She had always been praying that she would outlive Bernice. They both died on the Sabbath."

A Thanksgiving feast

—First published on Nov. 26, 1981

In December of 1621, Governor Bradford of the little colony of Plymouth, Mass., ordered a day of thanks.

The Pilgrims had suffered through a year of hunger and cold, a year of sickness and death. Their food supply had dwindled. But the Pilgrims endured, and they had harvested a bountiful crop.

Governor Bradford directed members of his colony to enter the forests to harvest turkeys, partridges and wood pigeons.

The feast day, he announced, would be Dec. 13. Five women from the colony directed the plucking, dressing and roasting of the turkeys, the broiling of the fish, the making of barley bread and cornbread, and the baking of pumpkin pies.

A runner went to Mount Hope to invite Indians there to the Thanksgiving feast.

And on Dec. 13, shortly after Captain Standish fired off his gun at sunrise, the Indians arrived, carrying deer and other food.

The Indians and the Pilgrims feasted together, in friendly fashion—America's first Thanksgiving celebration.

The participants in that first Thanksgiving could hardly have imagined the controversy that over the years would accompany the tradition they initiated.

In 1939, for instance, President Franklin D. Roosevelt proclaimed that Thanksgiving would be celebrated on the fourth Thursday in November.

Thanksgiving traditionally had been celebrated the last Thursday of November, but in 1939, Roosevelt wanted to perk up the economy, he wanted to get cash registers ringing again, he wanted to help get America out of its Depression. Having Thanksgiving on the fourth Thursday would add a week to the Christmas shopping season—in 1939, no one thought of beginning Christmas shopping until after Thanksgiving.

Almost half of the nation rose up to protest. Twenty-three of the 48 states decided to ignore Roosevelt; they would celebrate Thanksgiving on the last Thursday of the month.

Minnesota Gov. Harold Stassen urged his state to stick with the last-Thursday tradition. Stassen was a Republican and he may have been playing politics with a Democratic president, but he insisted he was determined to "keep sacred things sacred."

So while President Roosevelt and the people in 25 states sat down to turkey on Nov. 23 that year, Stassen and the people in 23 states waited; they would feast one week later.

In both 1940 and in 1941, Roosevelt proclaimed the fourth Thursday of November as Thanksgiving Day. Finally, Congress voted to permanently establish Thanksgiving on the last Thursday of November, and we have been following that tradition faithfully ever since.

Twenty-three years after the Pilgrims first celebrated Thanksgiving, the governor of the Dutch colony of New York issued the first Thanksgiving proclamation.

Congress recommended a day of Thanksgiving each year during the Revolutionary War. But after peace arrived in 1784, there was no national call for a day of thanks until Washington in 1789 ordered a day of Thanksgiving for the adoption of the Constitution. That was the first Thanksgiving proclamation issued by a president.

James Madison in 1818 set a day to give thanks for peace, and Abraham Lincoln in both 1862 and 1863 recommended special days of thanks for victories.

Lincoln in 1863 was the first president to proclaim Thanksgiving for the last Thursday in November. He had received pressure from Sarah J. Hale, editor of the *Ladies Magazine* in Boston (her magazine later merged with *Godey's Lady's Book*) to get "the day of our American Thanksgiving positively settled."

When Lincoln finally issued his proclamation, it focused upon "the blessings of fruitful fields and healthful skies."

"In the midst of a civil war of unequal magnitude and severity, which has sometimes seemed to foreign states to invite and provoke their aggressions, peace has been preserved with all nations, order has been maintained, the laws have been respected and obeyed, and harmony has prevailed everywhere except in the theater of military conflict....

"I do, therefore, invite my fellow citizens in every part of the United States, and also those who are at sea and those who are sojourning in foreign lands, to set apart and observe the last Thursday of November next as a day of Thanksgiving and praise to our beneficent Father who dewelleth in the heavens. And I recommend to them that, while offering up ascriptions justly due to Him for such singular deliverances and blessings, they do also, with humble penitence for our national perverseness and disobedience, commend to His tender care all those who have become widows, orphans, mourners or sufferers in the lamentable civil strife in which we are unavoidably engaged, and fervently implore the interposition of the almighty hand to heal the wounds of the nation and to restore it, as soon as may be consistent with the Divine purposes, to the full enjoyment of peace, harmony, tranquility and union."

It's that tradition that we continue today.

The Mankato hanging

—First published on Oct. 13, 1983

On Dec. 6, 1862, President Abraham Lincoln notified Col. Henry H. Sibley that Sibley should "cause to be executed" 39 of the 303 Santee Indians who had been convicted of participating in attacks against Southern Minnesota settlers.

"The other condemned prisoners you will hold subject to further orders," Lincoln wrote, "taking care that they neither escape nor are subjected to any unlawful violence."

Government authorities set the executions for Dec. 26, "in the Moon when the Deer Shed Their Horns," as Dee Brown wrote in *Bury My Heart at Wounded Knee.*

"That morning," Brown wrote, "the town of Mankato was filled with vindictive and morbidly curious citizens. A regiment of soldiers marched in to keep order. At the last minute, one Indian was given a reprieve. About 10 o'clock, the 38 condemned men were marched from the prison to the scaffold.

"They sang the Sioux death song until soldiers pulled white caps over their heads and placed nooses around their necks. At a signal from an army officer, the control rope was cut and 38 Santee Sioux dangled lifeless in the air.

"But for the intercession of Abraham Lincoln, there would have been 300; even so, a spectator boasted that it was 'America's greatest mass execution.'"

The mass execution is also one centerpiece in the *Emigrant Saga,* a merging of the books "Immigrants" and "The New Land." The *Emigrant Saga* is an excellent capsulization of some early American history, acted out in the beautiful, rustic setting of our countryside.

Part of the visual and emotional strength of *Saga* is that it forces us to watch as the 38 Indians are herded onto the scaffold, as the soldiers place the white cloth bags over their heads, as the soldiers fasten the nooses around their necks.

In *Saga,* the Indians stand in a rectangle, along the edges of a hanging platform. At the slicing of the rope, the edges of the platform collapse inward and the 38 Indians on all four sides drop into the air, dangling from ropes fastened to the heavy wooden beams above the gallows.

In *Saga,* not all of them hang lifeless. A few kick in the air for a few seconds, a few jerk spasmodically as nerves react to the life being choked out of the bodies.

■

The Mankato execution also was on the mind of Nelson Big Crow when he came to Mankato this month. He came here from St. Francis, S.D., and he said he's planning to sue the city of Mankato because it was the site of the hangings.

"I certify that I will file suit papers on aforesaid town of Mankato, Minn., 56001, for hanging 38 Sioux forefathers," Big Crow wrote in a note.

Big Crow said he planned to sue the city for $1 million for each Indian hanged here. He said he doesn't want the money for himself, but says he will ask that the money be used to set up a scholarship fund for other Sioux.

"This is just one man's effort alone," Big Crow said. "I've made it before, and I'm going to make it again."

Big Crow, who says he's a veteran of conflicts in both Korea and Vietnam and who calls himself "a veteran and a warrior," said he wanted to bring the suit because his Sioux brothers "fought for freedom, just like you and I. They fought for freedom, and they lost."

■

In truth, if Big Crow wants to pursue any legal action, he probably will have to pursue it against the federal government.

A five-man military commission had tried the Indians who had participated in the 1862 Sioux uprising.

Many of the Sioux prisoners ended up being convicted by the testimony of Joseph Godfrey. Godfrey, a mulatto born of a black mother and a French-Canadian father, had been the first prisoner tried. He had been found guilty of murder and had been sentenced "to be hanged by the neck until he is dead." Commission members agreed to commute his sentence to 10 years in prison if he testified against other Sioux in the uprising.

In a book entitled *The Sioux Uprising of 1862* published by the Minnesota Historical Society, author Kenneth Carley writes that "reading the records today buttresses the impression that the trials were a travesty of justice."

"It is true that those in charge had to resist public pressure to do away with all the Indians, guilty and innocent alike, and it must also be pointed out that the trials were conducted by a military commission and not by a court of law. Nevertheless, many of the proceedings were too hasty and quite a number of prisoners were condemned on flimsy evidence.

"Many Indians who had expected to be treated as prisoners of war were sentenced to death merely for being present at such battles as New Ulm and Birch Coulee. As soon as a prisoner admitted firing a shot at whites, no matter where, the commission with unseemly haste sentenced him to hang."

Brown wrote in *Wounded Knee* that just hours after the hangings, "officials discovered that two of the men hanged were not on Lincoln's list," but nothing was said about that for nine years.

Brown wrote: "'It was a matter of regret that any mistakes were made,' declared one of those responsible. 'I feel sure they were not made intentionally.'

"One of the innocent men hanged had saved a white woman's life during the raiding."

The Elephant Man

—First published on Nov. 20, 1980

He was an older man, trim but with tangled white hair, wearing work clothes that hung from rather than fit his body, and walking in scruffy work shoes.

He was trying to cross Broad Street in Mankato, Minn., just as I was. We had been brought together suddenly by the heavy traffic that kept both of us poised on the curb.

The man struck up a conversation, startling me: here was a fellow, without invitation, interrupting my morning meditation. Rather than feeling a kinship, I found myself slightly taken aback: first, people walking along the streets of a city even this size don't often speak to one another; secondly, he needed a barber and a better tailor.

We walked together, with the man doing most of the talking and me doing most of the listening, until he turned toward the bus depot and his morning meal.

That encounter from a few days ago started stirring in my mind after I saw *The Elephant Man.*

And I had to ask, would I have reacted differently had that man been distinguished as well as trim, well-dressed as well as friendly? Sadly, I had to admit, I'm sure I would have.

The Elephant Man tells the story based on fact about John Merrick (Joseph Merrick, some say), a young man horribly disfigured by a condition known as neurofibromatosis.

I cannot remember a movie in recent years that chewed on my nerve endings like this one.

I found it a sensitive, effective film. When it had ended, I just sat there for a moment, trying to figure out why the cruelty Merrick found in Victorian London had affected me so deeply.

I felt good knowing a sensitive, intelligent being inhabited this disfigured face and misshapen body. But I was saddened by the ridicule and cruelty he had been forced to endure—and further saddened that had I seen him on the street, I likely would have shunned him just as everyone else did.

Seven years ago in Mundelein, Ill., I interviewed a man named Peter Risch.

He was 30 years old, and he was 32 inches tall.

Sitting in the living room of the home where Risch and his mother lived, I tried to prepare myself for the moment this man would walk into the room.

But my preparation wasn't nearly good enough. I can still remember feeling a little light-headed when Risch walked in. He was the smallest man I'd ever seen, and I'm sure the expression on my face displayed my feelings completely.

Risch, I assume, was used to this. And he played the perfect host, allowing me to recover while he settled into his tiny chair.

Before long, we were chatting away like old friends. And it helped me realize we were really quite alike, after all.

Risch told me he loved to walk up to the little people at circuses or at state fairs, especially those who claimed to be "The Smallest Man in the World." "They're always taller than I am," he said.

Risch talked candidly about dating girls. He did not discriminate, he said—he dated "regular-sized girls" as well as those his own size. "They all have the same equipment," he said.

And Risch talked about cruelty, about how both adults and children often made fun of him or shouted abusive comments as he walked in Mundelein.

Memories of the encounter with Risch also started stirring after seeing *The Elephant Man.* The messages were similar: very fine and very sensitive people come in quite different packages, and exterior appearances should not dictate how we treat them.

A church bulletin I picked up Sunday carried thoughts that, though more pious than I would write, pulled the whole subject together.

I'm not sure who wrote the words, but they jumped out at me from the page.

"To manage and plan and control life in such a way that there is room only for 'friends' who do not disrupt one's plans and expectations is to keep God out of one's life.

"The 'unwanted' child, the physically deformed, the senile, even the morally deformed criminal are all unwelcome by human standards, but faith makes room for them because faith knows instinctively that life pertains to the essence of divine mystery, and that mystery is to be welcomed and entertained, not rejected and destroyed."

Pearl Harbor veteran

—First published on Dec. 8, 1981

The first Japanese plane, a dive bomber, streaked in low from the south at 7:55 a.m.

Other bombers in the same unit swung wide around the west coast of Oahu and dove in on U.S. Army bombers lined up neatly on Hickam Field. Bombers in a second unit swerved to the right and, from the north, attacked U.S. fighter planes standing on Wheeler Field.

Immediately behind those first units, 40 torpedo bombers skimmed just above Pearl Harbor, and unleashed their weapons on the ships in Battleship Row.

In the wake of the Japanese torpedo planes came 50 horizontal bombers, helping to assure the success of the first wave. Last came 45 fighters, to gun down any U.S. planes that might get into the air and to polish off any remaining planes at Wheeler and Hickam.

This massive Japanese force was flung within the space of a few minutes at virtually every prominent naval and air installation on Oahu. Within the first 15 minutes of the attack, the Japanese had successfully destroyed or paralyzed virtually the entire air strength on Oahu—the U.S. planes, defueled and packed tightly into neat rows so they could be more closely guarded against sabotage, proved easy targets.

In less than an hour, the Japanese moved alarmingly close to their main objectives—crippling U.S. air power in the Pacific and destroying the U.S. Navy's Pacific fleet.

When the first Japanese plane came in, Victor Paradis, who lives at 1426 Carney Ave. in Mankato, Minn., was standing at attention, waiting for the U.S. flag to be raised at the U.S. Navy's submarine base on Oahu.

Paradis had been assigned to work in the engine room of the Northampton, a heavy cruiser; but now, for several weeks, he would be attending machinist school at the submarine base.

Four other men and Paradis saw the first torpedo plane swing into the harbor.

One of the men spotted the red suns on the fuselage of the first bomber and hollered, "My God, that's not our plane!"

The plane flew low, about 500 feet above the water, Paradis remembers, and he and his friends could see the pilot.

The submarine base was about a mile from Battleship Row, but Paradis, then age 22, recalls how vividly he and his friends could see the attack.

The torpedo bombers "had to come in real low" to drop their torpedoes into the water.

"I actually saw the live torpedoes as they were dropped, heading towards the water and the battleships."

The Japanese pilots were drawing barrages of anti-aircraft gunfire. But most of the noise that Dec. 7 came from torpedoes exploding.

"We could see the fire, and the smoke just belching out of the ships."

The Japanese hit several ships—the Maryland, the Utah, the Tennessee, the Arizona, the West Virginia, the Oklahoma, the California, the Nevada. Every battleship except the Pennsylvania, which was in dry-dock, sustained some heavy damage. Three cruisers, the Raleigh, the Helena and the Honolulu, sustained serious damage.

The lives of 2,086 Navy servicemen and 237 Army servicemen were lost.

The entire U.S. base had been caught off guard, Paradis admits. "Normally, Sunday morning is a very lax day." By the time the servicemen had collected themselves, the Japanese were gone.

The submarine base where Paradis worked had been untouched. Navy men there "drew rifles, in case there had been a landing by the Japanese."

Paradis and others began helping soldiers who had been wounded during the attack.

Many of those injured were brought to the submarine base, to a small hospital containing about 25 beds.

The survivors drew his sympathy, Paradis said. "Some were half-clothed. Some just had their underclothes on, or just a pair of pants on."

Some of the men had jumped over the sides of the burning ships and had been picked up by smaller boats in the harbor.

"Some of their eyes were all red from the fuel oil they had to swim through."

Paradis belongs to the Pearl Harbor Survivors Association.

He and his wife Lucille and six other couples from the Mankato area are in Hawaii this week for the group's 40th-year reunion in Hawaii. They will be there eight days, joining about 5,000 other members, the largest gathering yet for the group.

Paradis will spend much of that time reminiscing with other service members, who were at Pearl Harbor on the day the United States was drawn into the war in the Pacific.

Paradis, like the others, went on to other action in the war—serving on one of the ships that escorted the aircraft carriers Enterprise and Hornet (Jimmy Doolittle's wing took off from the Hornet for its attack on Tokyo); serving on a ship in the Battle of the Midway and watching the aircraft carrier Wasp go down; and watching his own ship, the Northampton, which he had rejoined after machinist school, go down, the victim of three torpedoes fired from a Japanese destroyer off the coast of Guadalcanal.

Of all of his experiences, of course, Paradis most remembers Pearl Harbor.

He's very aware of the debate that has raged over whether the Japanese really paralyzed the U.S. fleet as much as the Americans and the Japanese at first thought.

Paradis says the Japanese could have devastated the United States' Pacific operation even more had they followed the air strike with a land invasion of Oahu.

"If the Japanese actually knew the effectiveness of their raid," he says, "well, it could have made a difference in the war."

Memories from The Met

—First published on Dec. 17, 1981

When the Minnesota Vikings clash with the Kansas City Chiefs on Sunday, Metropolitan Stadium will hold its last capacity crowd.

After the people leave and after the stadium breathes its last, we will be left only with the memory of athletes making their mark in this park: Harmon Killebrew powering home runs; Rod Carew stealing home; Fran Tarkenton scrambling for first downs; Ahmad Rashad making miracle catches.

Not many of those in the stands ever reached the field, to leave the own marks on the Met. But I did. The memory remains painful, but now is the appropriate time to pass along the story.

On Friday, June 10, 1960, St. James High School won its way into the state baseball tournament with a 5-4 win over Westbrook.

It took some days for the full impact to sink in—we would be playing baseball on Tuesday, June 21, at Metropolitan Stadium.

Ours was a scrappy team. We had only one senior, Michael Torkelson (who now works in St. Peter with the Minnesota School Boards Association).

We won games with pitching (Don Mickelson, now police chief at St. James, hadn't lost a game all year) and defense.

As *Mankato Free Press* sports editor Scott Nelson reported in his pre-tournament article, we had only three hitters above the .300 mark—I was playing first base and hitting .375, Steve Strommen (now a coach in the Bloomington School District) played third base and was hitting .333, and Don Anderson, our left fielder, was hitting .310.

Strommen had carried the big bat through the regional tournament, winning the last game for us with a three-run homer in the seventh and last inning. It was the only home run our team hit all season.

The first game of the tournament matched us against Little Falls.

Little Falls ultimately would be the tournament runner-up, but for four innings, we held a 1-0 lead. In the fifth inning, with the score now tied 1-1, Mickelson, who had been hurt a few days earlier when a line drive slammed into his foot, began to tire; the sore toe threw off his motion, and a relief pitcher had to be summoned. Little Falls scored six more times in the inning.

"Our youth and inexperience showed at times," Coach Arnold Veglahn told reporters after the game. "We lost five runners on the bases."

Torkelson, who had banged out a single and a double, agreed: "We got some good hits, but I got caught twice on the bases myself."

The following afternoon, we took the field against Austin.

Austin, a pre-tournament favorite, had been upset by Hutchinson the day before. Austin's players were angry.

The game went scoreless for the first two innings, then Austin erupted for five runs. Austin went on to score another run in the fifth, four in the sixth and eight in the seventh. The final: 18-1.

My contribution had been substantial. Of six strikeouts by Austin pitchers, three were mine. Of nine errors by St. James fielders, three were mine.

Most embarrassing of all, we couldn't get Austin out in the final inning. *The Free Press* sports reporter told the whole story: "Austin ended the final frame by walking the last two men off base and allowing them to be tagged out."

As we had moved into the final inning, Clayton Reed, something of an athletic legend at Austin, had stood beside me at first base after the last of his three hits. Reed also played first base. "Don't worry about it, kid," he tried to console me. "I can remember playing in the state tournament as a sophomore, and I can remember how nervous I was. You'll be back."

Reed was right. Two years later, we would be playing baseball in another state tournament, this time at Midway Stadium in St. Paul.

But today, as the Vikings approach their final game at Metropolitan Stadium, only that first state tournament matters.

Three strikeouts. Three errors. The final: 18-1.

A still vivid memory from The Met, may she rest in peace.

Praying for Bryan

—First published on Sept. 22, 1981

Bryan Zyskowski has a colorful poster taped to the wall above his bed.

It features a large squirrel, and a message that reads, "God will provide."

The poster came for Bryan while he was at the Mayo Clinic in Rochester. He had his left leg amputated in February after doctors found cancer, and a young friend hoped the poster would speed Bryan's recovery.

Bryan received other cards and gifts, too—lots of them. With the money in some of the cards, Bryan bought a water bed that has helped him sleep with less pain and a stereo that he plays almost constantly.

Bryan's parents, James and Marilyn Zyskowski, 418 Monroe Ave., say the outpouring of good wishes for their 10-year-old son has been satisfying, but not surprising.

"He's an all-American boy—into everything," Mrs. Zyskowski says. "He enjoys doing everything."

He's outgoing, and he makes friends easily, she says. "He has more friends than the rest of us might ever hope to have."

Last week, Bryan helped raise money to buy new physical education equipment at Trinity Christian School, 100 Garfield Ave.

Bryan and 46 other students participated in a marathon run around Spring Lake Park. The students went about 200 miles to raise more than $2,000. Bryan, riding in a motor-driven wheelchair, went around the course three times to bring in about $200.

"He was very tired after three times," his mother said. "That was the first physical activity he has been involved in for some time."

The marathon raised enough money for the physical education equipment. Any extra money will be used to buy a film strip projector.

The cancer in Bryan's left leg was first discovered in January.

"Last fall," Mrs. Zyskowski said, "he would play football and he would fall down."

In January, after his problem worsened, Bryan went to a doctor, and osteogenic sarcoma, a rare form of bone cancer, was diagnosed.

In February, he underwent surgery.

Since Bryan's amputation, additional cancer cells have been detected in his body, primarily above his legs and in his lungs.

This month he completed intensive cobalt treatments at Immanuel-St. Joseph Hospital. He underwent three weeks of treatments, followed by three weeks of rest, then three more weeks of treatment. The 28 treatments of 5,000 rads "knocked him flat," his mother says.

The cobalt treatments also cut his appetite. That's now the Zyskowskis' prime concern. They hope that vitamins and minerals can be prescribed to keep Bryan strong—until his appetite returns.

"All things considered, he's got a fantastic attitude," his father says. "He'll be back in school as soon as his appetite picks up."

Because of his illness, Bryan missed half of his classes last school year.

Even at that, however, he did well in his studies. In math, for example, he finished at the head of his class.

"He keeps coming in when he feels up to it," says Peter Hunt, administrator at Trinity Christian School. "He's keeping up with his school work at home, concentrating on the three R's, of course."

Mrs. Zyskowski has taught at Trinity, so she helps Bryan when she can. District 77 also will pick up the tab for Bryan to have a tutor one hour per school day, but Bryan hasn't been strong enough this school year to take advantage of that.

Though Bryan continues to suffer a lot of pain, the Zyskowskis and their two other children, Jeff, 15, and Julie, 8, try to keep him as active as possible.

"If he feels good," Mrs. Zyskowski says, "we take advantage of it."

The Christmas before his cancer was discovered, Bryan had received a new dirt bike. When he returned home from the hospital, he was determined to ride the bike—and he did. With a special strap for his foot, he can ride around his block in North Mankato. He also roller-skates, rides horses, fishes, listens to music and works on his skills as an artist.

"He's very artistic, and very creative," his mother says. "He likes the creative arts."

"When he's up and going," his father says, "you don't have to find things for him to do.

"He has an attitude that's very uplifting to us. He has no defeatist attitude at all."

A lot of people are pulling for Bryan.

People have called long distance to see how he's doing. People have dropped by the house to visit.

"We know there are people praying for him across the United States," Mrs. Zyskowski says. "We have not given up hope. We know that God does answer prayer."

Bryan's battle has helped all the family members better appreciate what they have, Bryan's father says.

"We have been blessed, miraculously.

"We don't look at tomorrow. We look at today." For Bryan and Bryan's family, he says, "every day is a new day."

Bryan—he's free at last

—First published on Oct. 27, 1981

Bryan Zyskowski's family and Bryan Zyskowski's friends said goodbye to him Sunday.

Bryan, 10, the son of James and Marilyn Zyskowski, 418 Monroe St., had battled the cancer in his body since earlier this year when doctors discovered it in his left leg.

Bryan's body lost that battle, and he died Thursday at his home.

But for about 300 people who crowded into Trinity Christian Church at Sherman Street and Webster Avenue, Bryan hadn't lost at all.

He had found his way to a better place, and, in the process, he had shown them how to live.

Poignant testimonials came from four of Bryan's friends at Trinity Christian School. They spoke for a few moments, all struggling mightily with their emotions as they reflected on their lives with Bryan.

"Bryan and I were close friends," said Anthony Welman, a fifth-grader. "We used to ride bikes. I've known him for about eight years." When Anthony could not go on, Pastor Cleon Laughlin said, "We know how you feel."

Wendy Darge, a sixth-grader who first met Bryan last year during orientation day, recalled Bryan's athletic abilities. "He always tried hardest to have his team win," she said. "He was always the first one picked when we picked teams. The one thing I remember about Bryan was that he was happy no matter what."

Brenda Bennett, a fifth-grader, said Bryan had not been able to come to school this year because of his illness. But last year, she remembered, Bryan had come to school to take a math test. "And wouldn't you know it, Bryan got the highest score in the class."

Brenda said Bryan's example meant a lot to her. "Now, when I get a bump or a bruise, I think of Bryan, and I don't cry as much."

Roy Schweim, a sixth-grader, echoed that: "He's put an imprint on my life. He was a good friend. He accepted things as they were."

The cancer in Bryan's left leg had been discovered in January.

Doctors diagnosed it as osteogenic sarcoma, a rare type of bone cancer. In February, Bryan underwent surgery to have his leg amputated.

A few weeks after the amputation, additional cancer cells were found in Bryan's body, primarily above his legs and in his lungs. He had undergone cobalt treatments. The 28 treatments had "knocked him flat," his mother said, and they cut his appetite.

Bryan suffered from the pain, but his brother Jeff, 15, and his sister Julie, 8, tried to keep him active.

"If he feels good," his mother said last month, "we take advantage of it."

It eventually became necessary for Bryan to take medication to ease his pain, however, and he spent much of the last month in his room at home, resting and sleeping.

Through Bryan's illness, the Zyskowski family and their friends held to a faith that Bryan might be cured.

Bryan shared that hope. "He has an attitude that's very uplifting to us," Bryan's father said last month. "He has no defeatist attitude at all."

That positive faith pervaded the service on Sunday. Pastor Laughlin called it a celebration—"It is a precious time when a child of God comes home."

Peter Hunt, principal at Trinity Christian School, said that "really, deep down, it's tears of joy, of contentment, because Bryan is free at last."

That was the theme of the tribute the Zyskowski family wrote for Bryan.

"Bryan is free at last from the prison his body has held him in," they said.

"His spirit has soared to new heights as it winged its way toward its final destination—an eternity with Jesus that Bryan prepared for and welcomed with increasing anticipation.

"He now realizes the fulfillment of his own admission verbalized early in his struggle—'It doesn't matter what happens to my body, Mom. It's what's inside that counts.'"

Hurry up and get old

—First published on Sept. 23, 1982

Catch Esther Gareis when she's sitting still, and you can gather sound advice for good living at age 77.

"How much rust I collect on my joints is going to be up to me," she says. "I want to wear out, not rust out.

"Think of something you can do for someone, even if it's just giving them a smile or a pat on the back....Cast your bread upon the waters and it comes back buttered—sometimes even with a bit of jelly.

"A man told me this morning, 'Esther, I've never seen you when you didn't smile at people.' Talk about getting your bouquets while you can smell them."

It's not easy to catch Mrs. Gareis sitting still. She's on the lecture circuit urging senior citizens to stay active to stay healthy, and she's setting a frenetic example for them.

"Live it up," the New Ulm, Minn., woman tells her listeners. "It's later than you think. Decide to make the most of every day. This should be the best period of your life.

"I believe in exercise. How do I practice what I preach? I'm keeping physically and mentally active. I still spend 30 minutes every morning doing Jack La Lanne's exercises." Turn the heads and stretch the necks, she says. Left. Right. Forward. Bend forward in the chair. Up. Down. Sideways.

"I fight the battle of the bulge. Five years ago, I decided to change from a size 20 dress to a 14. I learned how to do it on the Weight Watcher's program, and now for four years I haven't varied more than a pound or two. I realize if I gain it back I'm hurting no one but myself."

Mrs. Gareis came to the New Ulm area, to Klossner, in 1924. "I came to teach," she says, "and married a farmer."

She was a farm homemaker for 21 years, and she and her husband had two daughters. "They were ages 7 and 9 when their father had a heart attack." The attack was fatal: he died at age 46.

Mrs. Gareis turned the family farm over to a farm management service and returned to teaching for 11 years.

She then remarried, she says, "and hit the jackpot." She married Walter J. Gareis, a New Ulm banker who "wanted to travel." And travel they did, extensively, from 1959 on—across the continental United States, to Hawaii and Guam, into Europe and Africa.

"We did pretty much the whole world," Mrs. Gareis says. "We didn't visit Australia, though, even though he had friends there. We put it off too long."

Most lavish was a 4½-month visit to Europe in 1966, a trip that cost the Gareises just under $6,000.

After her second husband died, Mrs. Gareis remained active.

Her interests continued to include 4-H, Girl Scouts, the New Ulm Golden Age Club, the New Ulm Hospital Auxiliary, the Red Cross Blood Bank and the United Way Fund. She helped establish the Golden Age Club in 1965 and helped organize the Dinners for Shut-ins program in 1972.

"Let's keep our people in their homes as long as we can," is her battle cry for the Dinners for Shut-ins (now Meals on Wheels) program. "I can't do all the work myself, but I've been fortunate to find people who will help." Each day, volunteers from a pool of 100 people deliver meals to 50 shut-ins.

In 1973, Mrs. Gareis received the New Ulm Sertoma Club's Service to Mankind Award. In 1976, she was named Brown County Senior Citizen of the Year, then went on to become Minnesota Senior Citizen of the Year.

In 1977, Mrs. Gareis spoke to the Governor's Council on Aging. Her topic: "Hurry Up and Get Old."

"It's the best time of your life," she said.

"There are many good things about getting old. Responsibilities are less. Commitments are fewer. You don't have to prove yourself. You don't have to compete. You don't have to have a purpose for everything you do—like taking a walk in the woods without looking for mushrooms."

There's more time to help others, Mrs. Gareis said. She told of a call to help a patient who needed transportation from the New Ulm Medical Clinic to the hospital. "I dropped what I was doing and took him to the hospital. In half an hour, I had completed my 'errand of mercy' and was home, feeling great because I was able to help. It was really selfish of me. Look what it had done for me. I had made a new friend. I had a pleasant break in my day."

Senior citizens must learn to "accept and adjust," Mrs. Gareis says. That's one of her favorite bits of wisdom. Another, one she has written on the cover of her phone book so she's sure to see it each day, goes, "When you get up in the morning, decide to be happy."

"I've always had my nose in everything," Mrs. Gareis says. "I am busy. I am involved.

"I'm healthy, and I'm having such a good time."

Know your presidents

—First published on Oct. 9, 1980

Presidential candidates tempted to deliver long speeches should consider the fate of William Henry Harrison.

Harrison, our ninth president, delivered the longest inaugural address in our nation's history—8,443 words.

But his marathon exposure to the elements that day brought Harrison a cold, and he died of pneumonia after only one month in office. His was the shortest term ever served by a U.S. president.

Such presidential trivia has been flowing freely during campaign 1980.

Some other tasty morsels:

■ Thomas Jefferson was one of our most spirited presidents, running up a $10,000 wine tab during his eight-year stay in the White House.

■ Jefferson was friendly in other ways, too. He initiated the tradition of shaking hands at White House receptions. Theodore Roosevelt established the record for presidential handshaking, however, when he greeted 8,315 people one-by-one on New Year's Day in 1907.

■ William Howard Taft was the largest White House occupant, standing 6 feet tall and weighing well over 300 pounds. After he got stuck in his bathtub on a couple of occasions, he finally ordered a specially built tub large enough to hold four average-sized men.

■ John Adams and John F. Kennedy drew raves for their reading abilities—Adams read fluently in seven languages, Kennedy could read 2,000 words per minute with almost total comprehension.

■ Gerald Ford served as both president and vice president without winning election. He was appointed vice president in 1973 after Spiro Agnew resigned, and he became president the following year when Richard Nixon resigned.

■ Nixon was the only president forced to leave the White House in disgrace. Sportsmen can point out that Nixon also was the only president who neither hunted nor fished.

■ John Tyler may have been our most active president. He was the father of 15 children.

Why would anyone want to be elected president in 1980, author William Oscar Johnson asked.

"Since 1940, no U.S. president in a year ending in a zero has come out of the Oval Office alive," Johnson wrote in his book, *The Zero Factor.*

His list:

■ William Henry Harrison, elected in 1840, died of pneumonia in 1841.

■ Abraham Lincoln, elected in 1860, was assassinated in 1865.

■ James A. Garfield, elected in 1880, was assassinated in 1881.

■ William McKinley, elected in 1900, died of a gunshot wound in 1901.

■ Warren G. Harding, elected in 1920, died following a stroke in 1923.

■ Franklin D. Roosevelt, elected in 1940, died of a cerebral hemorrhage in 1945.

■ John F. Kennedy, elected in 1960, was assassinated in 1963.

Columnist Donald Kaul of the *Des Moines Register* takes that topic a step further.

Not only did these presidents die in office, he writes, but "...they are the *only* American presidents to die in office, unless you count Zachary Taylor, which hardly anyone ever does."

Kaul also asks what John Tyler, Andrew Johnson, Chester A. Arthur, Theodore Roosevelt, Calvin Coolidge, Harry Truman and Lyndon Johnson all had in common. In addition to being president, each was elected vice president at the start of a decade.

"Not one of them was chosen because of his known statesmanlike qualities or even with the thought that he might someday become president. They were accidents, all of them."

Unfortunately for Kaul, he missed the mark on at least two of those men. Andrew Johnson became vice president in 1865, Harry Truman became vice president in 1945. They did succeed new-decade presidents who died in office, granted, but they were not elected with those presidents at the beginning of the decade.

We're having a cold snap

—First published on Sept. 25, 1980

Laura said nothing: she was too happy. She could hardly believe that the winter was gone, that spring had come. When Pa asked her why she was so silent, she answered soberly, "I said it all in the night."

—The Long Winter
By Laura Ingalls Wilder

Indian Legend says that every seventh winter will be a tough one.

Indian legend also says that at the end of three times seven comes the hardest winter of all.

One of those hardest of all winters occurred in 1880-1881, the year Laura Ingalls Wilder details in *The Long Winter.*

Jan Evans of 113 Swiss St. in Mankato, Minn., is an avid reader of Laura Ingalls Wilder, and she suggested that I read *The Long Winter,* following my note here last week that this year marks the centennial anniversary of one of Minnesota's longest and stormiest winters ever.

The winter of 1880-1881, she said, was not only long and cold in Minnesota, but throughout the Midwest.

In *The Long Winter,* Pa moves the Ingalls family to town, following a warning from an Indian.

"I feel like hurrying," Pa tells Mrs. Ingalls early in the book. "I'm like the muskrat. Something tells me to get you and the girls inside thick walls. I've been feeling this way for some time, and now that Indian…."

Blizzards soon snowed the little town under, cutting off all supplies from the outside.

The first blizzard struck in October, and it was May before all the snow melted—a winter of eight months, a winter so long it left Laura nearly speechless, though happy, when she realized it was over. "I said it all in the night," she said—in the night, she had observed the Chinook winds carrying spring.

"Winter had lasted so long," Laura wrote of her family, "that it seemed it would never end. It seemed that they would never really wake up."

Mrs. Evans points out that if every seventh year brings a hard winter, the next hard winter should occur in 1985-1986, 105 years after The Long Winter. That winter of 1985-1986 should also be the hardest of all winters, the one that comes at the end of three times seven years.

■

In predicting a long, cold winter this year, I mentioned that one observer had spotted woolly-bear caterpillars with wide black bands. That indicates a brutal winter is in the offing.

Further, let me quote Helen Wohlschlaeger, a woman from St. Louis, who claims 100 percent accuracy during the 12 years she has been forecasting winters based upon the color of the woolly-bear caterpillar.

The caterpillars are black this year, she says. If a woolly-bear expects a severe winter, the creature's black bands grow thicker to better absorb heat. The thicker the bands, the worse the winter.

Mrs. Wohlschlaeger said a neighbor boy brought her a white woolly-bear caterpillar, and "it's getting darker and darker. My son Jimmy brought in an all-black one."

Jan Evans, from her Mankato vantage point, offered one more indicator of a cold winter this year—the muskrat huts have been exceptionally thick. Laura Ingalls Wilder would take that indicator quite seriously.

■

Finally, Don R. Marben, editor and publisher of the *Lake Crystal Tribune,* offers a further primer for predicting winters.

It's going to be a cold winter, he says, if you observe:

- Thicker than normal corn husks.
- Early arrival of a Snowy owl.
- Early migration of the monarch butterfly.
- Thick hair on the nape of the cow's neck.
- Raccoons with thick tails and bright bands.

- Spiders spinning larger than usual webs and entering the house in greater numbers.
- An unusual abundance of acorns.
- Squirrels gathering nuts early to fortify against a hard winter.
- Frequent halos or rings around the sun or moon.
- Muskrats burrowing holes high on the river bank.
- Woodpeckers sharing a tree.
- Narrow orange bands in the middle of the woolly-bear caterpillars.
- Fat and fuzzy woolly-bears.

Winter

o o o o o o o o o o o o o o o o o o o o o o o o o o o o o o

Whose woods these are I think I know.
His house is in the village though;
He will not see me stopping here
To watch his woods fill up with snow.
My little horse must think it queer
To stop without a farmhouse near
Between the woods and frozen lake
The darkest evening of the year.
He gives his harness bells a shake
To ask if there is some mistake.
The only other sound's the sweep
Of easy wind and downy flake.
The woods are lovely, dark and deep.
But I have promises to keep,
And miles to go before I sleep,
And miles to go before I sleep.

—Robert Frost
"Stopping By Woods On A Snowy Evening"

Homemade ice cream

—First published on Feb. 4, 1982

Once winter had gripped the farm firmly in its frozen fist, you could almost see the ice growing in the livestock water tank.

The cattle usually kept a spot open on one side, where they could dip their noses and lap up the icy liquid.

But when winter threatened to freeze even that spot, Dad would decide we had better crank out some ice cream.

Excitement grew once we heard the word.

We would struggle into our warmest clothes and pull on our old work gloves.

Then we would grab a gunnysack and an ax, and head for the frozen water tank.

Chipping out the ice was a challenge—the ax biting into ice sent tiny shards of frozen fragments toward our eyes; an extra-hard chop would break through the ice, sending the chilling water splashing into our faces; and care was necessary to keep the ax from glancing off the ice and into our shins.

When we had chopped out enough ice to fill our gunnysack, we dragged it to our house.

There we placed it on the front steps and pounded at it with a hammer. That reduced the chunks of ice to a manageable size. Once that was accomplished, we could move on to the churning.

We used a 5-quart metal container to hold the ice cream mixture.

While we had been chipping out the ice, Mom had been blending the ice cream ingredients in the metal container. The container, filled to the three-quarter mark, would be brought from the kitchen into the basement. There it would be placed inside a large wooden pail, and a metal crank would be fastened in place at the top.

The small pieces of ice were poured into the wooden pail, where they would rest around the walls of the metal container. Handfuls of rock salt would be tossed into the ice, to ensure that the ice would properly chill the ice cream.

Dad did most of the cranking. Whenever I cranked, I wore two work gloves, one on my hand holding the cover atop the ice cream container, so my hand wouldn't freeze, the other on the hand turning the crank, so my fingers wouldn't blister.

We turned the crank for a very long time, maybe half an hour, before it began pulling hard.

Once the mixture began to freeze, it thickened very fast, and Dad would finish the cranking—he was the only one who could turn the crank at the end.

Then we would pull the metal container out of the wooden pail, and Mom would carry it upstairs to the kitchen. There she would remove the cover and pull out the metal mixer, soft ice cream dripping from it into the sink.

The first taste for us came when we spooned the excess ice cream off the mixer. Then, if we were lucky, we'd each get a small bowl filled with the softest of the mixture.

The rest would go into the ice box, where it would freeze to the proper consistency for future desserts.

In our family, we still make homemade ice cream today.

The standard vanilla recipe we use came from Eldon Hovde, the fire chief in St. James, Minn., and something of an ice cream connoisseur.

Good for a gallon, the ingredients include: six eggs; two cups of sugar; two 13-ounce cans of Carnation condensed milk; two cups of whole milk; one cup of whipping cream; three tablespoons of vanilla, and a pinch of salt.

All you do is beat the eggs, then add the sugar and the rest of the ingredients. You can try your own experiments with chocolate syrup, strawberries, raspberries, nuts and so forth.

Our new method of cranking out ice cream lacks the nostalgia of the old farm method: the ice comes out of a plastic bag you can buy in a food store rather than out of the cattle watering tank; the mixer has an electric motor rather than a crank.

The new method probably is easier.

But on occasions when I've been back on the farm, I've pulled out the ax and the gunnysack and marched down to the old water tank to chip out some ice.

Dragging out the oil wooden pail, and the old crank, I can churn out a batch of ice cream, all the while remembering one of the wonderful things about growing up on a farm in a Minnesota winter.

Freezing on the farm

—First published on Jan. 19, 1982

We have survived two consecutive weekends of North Pole weather.

Following such an arctic stretch, it's fitting that we would receive in the mail from Bob Larson of Milaca, Minn., a cold-weather diary to warm our hearth. In his diary, Larson focuses on a "typical" week in his life as a farmer.

As winter drags on, farmers can only dream of warmer days filled with spring field work and dawn-to-dusk schedules.

Larson's diary should help them remember, come spring, why they won't miss this year's frigid winter.

Monday

The water tank froze up again. Tried to find five-section drag. It's probably under snow somewhere. Found a heifer dead in the small pole barn. Looks like she bloated. Must be something she ate. Called the vet. Put new cow in with the others. Vet came. Said heifer bloated. It must be something she ate. Paid vet $15. I said, if he wanted, he could have the heifer instead.

Called bank. Asked manager about getting a $20,000 loan. He laughed. I didn't. New cow got out. Put her back in and fixed fence. Dinner cold. Wife hot—late for hairdresser.

New cow out again. Used pickup to herd her back in. Found five-section drag. Fixed front tire and rim on pickup and called implement dealer to see if he would take a slightly bent up five-section drag in trade.

Started to spread manure. Broke apron on spreader. Had to shovel off by hand. Rendering truck came to pick up dead heifer. Now sows are out.

Tuesday

Spreader frozen solid. Will call Fritz and see if I can thaw it out in his garage. Need to spray pigs. Sprayer frozen solid. Put sprayer in bathtub to thaw it out.

Wife mad. Said she'll divorce me if I thaw out sprayer in her bathtub again. May take her up on it.

Wife mad. Car won't start. New cow sure looks peaked. Vet here. Said new cow sure looks peaked. If she gets worse, call him. Paid $15.

Called for truck to pick up ear corn. Said they'd be here after dinner. Came at 11:45.

Wife mad. Dinner cold. Mother-in-law waiting to go to town shopping. Broke hydraulic hose on tractor loader. Changed clothes. New cow out again. Took her to sales barn. Got $900 for her. Neighbors bought her. Cow I just sold back in my pasture. Fixed fence. Wife mad. Hogs out in back yard. Tipped her clothes basket. Chased them back in and fixed fence. Wife screaming. Says car on fire. Ripped pants jumping over hog fence. New spark plug wires, anti-freeze and radiator hose. $43.50 plus tax.

Called station for 300 gallons gasoline. Up 1 cent again. Wife back. Says we are going to eat at the restaurant at 6:30. Says I should get the lead out.

Cow that neighbor bought is back in my pasture again. Called neighbor. Wife mad. Washer acting up. Must be the controls. Had to finish by hand. Now hogs are in the front yard.

7:30 p.m. Wife still mad. I ate soup.

Wednesday

Bank called. Tractor note past due. Nobody laughed. Sent check. Wife mad. Washer overfilled again. Trash barrels full, too. Ran hot water in manure spreader to thaw it out. Wife mad. Car won't start. Sewer is frozen up again. Fixed washer, started car, emptied trash barrels and unplugged sewer. Sat in easy chair with dirty clothes on. Wife mad.

Thursday

Water froze up. Forgot water running in manure spreader yesterday. Boy, oh boy. Bank called. Check for tractor note bounced. I laughed. Manager didn't. Sold 10 hogs. Prices down $5. Put Knipco heater under manure spreader.

Friday

Tire blown out on frozen-up manure spreader. Got too hot. Called to see what a new spreader would cost. Bank called. Said he might consider that $20,000 loan if John Block raised the dairy supports. We both laughed.

Ag teacher was here. Says I ought to plant sunflowers instead of corn. Maybe get to be a millionaire like those farmers in neighboring towns. I told him he could plant the bloomin' things if they were such a good deal. Implement dealer called. Wanted to know how I got that drag so beat up. He wished he had seen it first.

Saturday

Hog house door froze shut. Put Knipco heater against it. Went downtown to café for coffee. Wife called. Says hog house on fire. Sure was. Garden hose froze up. Called fire department. Truck got stuck in driveway. Put out fire with wet sacks and snow. Insurance man called. Says hog house not on policy. Wife mad. Feeder pigs ate dog food on back porch.

Sunday

Car wouldn't start. We all squeezed into the pickup. Wife got grease on her new skirt. Wife mad. Same sermon as a month ago. Went to sleep half through. Snored. Wife mad again. Wife's folks here. Took kids bowling. Sun went down peaceful. Thank God this week is over.

Christmas in prison camp

—First published on Dec. 16, 1982

Reidar Dittmann does not like lutefisk.

Most native Norwegians don't, he insists. Since arriving in Minnesota in 1945, trying to politely parry invitations to dine on the "quivering fish" has proven a most difficult challenge for him.

"In Norway," says Dittmann, professor of art history and director of galleries at St. Olaf College, "we ate lutefisk only if there was absolutely nothing else for survival."

In fact, he says, his father used lutefisk to discipline five sons. "'If you don't settle down,' he'd say, 'I'm going to make you eat some lutefisk.' That would be enough to quiet me down for several hours."

Dittmann realized his lutefisk challenge the moment he climbed aboard the boat in 1945 for passage to the United States. He and other passengers shared space with more than 5,000 pounds of cod destined for "the Olson Fish Co. in Duluth."

There, the cod would be dumped into lye and converted into the delicacy required for those who "indulge in the strange ritual called eating lutefisk."

When he arrived in Northfield, Dittmann discovered that "at St. Olaf at Christmas, they serve Norwegian food." Between October and Christmas, whenever people invited Dittmann to dine, knowing he came from Norway, they delighted in serving him lutefisk.

Finally, Dittmann couldn't stomach any more, and he began to decline invitations.

But even that didn't solve the problem.

One day, after turning down a dinner invitation, he showed up late at the college cafeteria, where he could select any of the many foods offered.

The head cook greeted him as he moved through the line, but she appeared quite concerned, he recalled.

"We had lutefisk today," she told him, "but I'm afraid it's all gone."

With a quick sigh of relief, Dittmann feigned hurt. "Mrs. Ryan, you don't say."

Then the cook's eyes brightened. "But I saved you a plate!" And she thrust a platter into Dittmann's hands, a platter piled high with lutefisk.

Dittmann's world has not always been so light-hearted.

He spent three years—and three Christmases—from 1942 to 1944 in Nazi concentration camps.

Dittmann described those years Tuesday night when he spoke at St. Peter to members of the Southern Minnesota Administrative Management Society.

On Dec. 22, 1941, Dittmann was bringing home some food, including a large amount of pork, when Nazi patrols stopped him. They did not arrest him, but they confiscated all the food. That meant that the Dittmann family would not enjoy its traditional Christmas meal of roast pork.

Early the following year, the Nazis placed Dittmann in a concentration camp, along with 2,000 other students from Oslo University.

As Christmas approached, Dittmann prepared to celebrate the holiday with other prisoners.

Dittmann described the camp on Christmas Eve. In December, the sun rises in Norway about 10 a.m. and sets about 2 p.m. Dittmann can still remember the late afternoon light shimmering off the North Sea, beneath the clear, dark skies.

In the distance, church bells were pealing, a tradition in Norway during the holiday. Prisoners began singing "Beautiful Savior."

Even in the concentration camp, Dittmann recalls, the atmosphere made it "very easy to become like children at Christmas." Dittmann and the other prisoners retired, very much in the holiday mood.

At 3 a.m., however, four Nazi guards loudly threw open the barracks' door and shouted in German, "Where is Dittmann?" He was dragged, barefoot and wearing only light clothing, into the icy night.

"I knew for a fact that for some reason or other, I had been singled out for execution. I walked along, knowing what lay ahead."

Dittmann remembers feeling faint, and he pitched forward into the snow, unconscious. He came to moments later, with two soldiers dragging him along in the snow. They stood him up in front of some rocks, in an area used to execute prisoners.

The camp commander then opened the door of the headquarters building and looked down at the prisoner. "Merry Christmas, Dittmann," he smiled.

"Apparently, he and other camp officials had been talking, and they decided it would be nice to scare one of the camp prisoners." An interesting prank for Christmas Day. "For some reason, I was the one they chose."

Dittmann does hold some fond memories of his time in the concentration camps.

"As human beings," he said, "we have an unlimited ability to react to various situations."

His fondest memory runs to Christmas Day in 1943.

He and other prisoners had been working on a project under Nazi guard. They had received no food, only water, for three days.

Returning to camp on that third day, "we were lying in the boxcars more dead than alive."

When the prisoners dragged themselves into their barracks, they saw a long table covered with a white table cloth and saw food lining that table "from one end to the other."

"I remember thinking, 'I must have died.'"

Five days before Christmas, the Germans had decided to apprehend and place in prison the entire police force of Denmark. That country had agreed to peacefully submit to the plan, on the condition that the trainload of prisoners would be accompanied by a trainload of food from Denmark, "the food basket of the world."

Hearing of Dittmann and 149 other starving Norwegian prisoners, the Danes had decided, "Let's celebrate our Christmas with them."

Dittmann and the other prisoners, nearly delirious with hunger, plunged toward the food. Take it easy, the Danes told them, or you will become sick. "There's more," they said.

That generosity, the people of one country sharing their wealth with the people of another, was in the true spirit of Christmas, and it left a lasting impression on Dittmann. "It is something I have never forgotten."

A casualty of Vietnam

—First published on March 4, 1980

Early in December of 1967, Wayne Bertilson received a letter from Odin Laingen, then 7th District congressman from Minnesota.

Laingen had been visiting Vietnam, and he had run across the 21-year-old soldier in South Vietnam's 3rd Field Hospital.

Bertilson, recovering from his second wound of the war, had written a note thanking the congressman for talking with him. Laingen's response emphasized that the young soldier "shouldn't be thanking us. Rather, we should be thanking you for the fine service you are performing for your country."

Early in December of 1979, Bertilson spent several days gathering signatures of Mankato residents to show support for the hostages in Iran. He wanted to send a card with those signatures at Christmastime so the hostages would know U.S. citizens were thinking about them.

Emil and Bess Bertilson of LaSalle said neither of those actions by their son surprised them. As Pastor John P. Trom of the LaSalle Lutheran Church said at Bertilson's funeral last week, "Many of us heard only about Wayne's being in trouble. We didn't hear about the good things, about the many people he helped."

It was fitting that on the funeral memorial, his age would be written out to the day—33 years, 3 months, 25 days. It seemed a reflection, somehow, of Bertilson's concern about the American hostages in Iran, and of the daily vigil U.S. citizens have kept ever since their captivity began 122 days ago.

Wayne Bertilson was a good friend.

He was three grades behind me in school, but he was a gifted baseball player, a pitcher his father once described as throwing "like a rifle."

We played together on St. James town teams two summers. When I played first base, my gloved hand would be raw after handling his pickoff throws. His pickoff throws had almost as much velocity as his bullets to batters.

We also served in Vietnam about the same time, although we were at opposite ends of the country—I was with the 1st Air Cavalry near Hue and Quang Tri in the north; he was with the 9th Infantry Division in the dangerous Delta region of the south.

Bertilson suffered wounds twice in the same leg, and the two wounds left a cross on the outside of his left thigh. They brought him two purple hearts, one presented by Hubert H. Humphrey. Humphrey wrote him a letter praising his service to his country.

Bertilson also received some psychological wounds. His first wound occurred when his point man stepped on a land mine and some of the shrapnel hit Bertilson; the point man didn't make it. Later, while Bertilson was on a week's leave in Thailand, his unit got hit very hard, and several of his best friends were either killed or wounded.

When Bertilson was scheduled to return home on Feb. 24, 1968, he told his mother that he didn't "want any fuss—no parades or anything like that."

"Well, he didn't have to worry about parades," she said, speaking of the anti-war sentiment that existed then.. "There wouldn't be any."

Upon returning home, Bertilson quickly discovered the unpopularity of the Vietnam war.

"He figured he was a hero when he was there," his father said. "But when he came back from Vietnam, people couldn't have cared less."

Bertilson had attended Mankato State University for two years, from 1965 to 1967, before being drafted. When he returned to school after his discharge, the anti-war protesting was intense.

"I think he'd have been a lot better if he hadn't gone back to college right away," his mother said.

The student protests had a great impact upon Bertilson. Though a bright and articulate young man who cared about people, he seemed to fall victim to what psychologists today call "delayed stress" in war veterans.

Bertilson turned to alcohol, to drugs, and to crime.

He was convicted of a number of burglaries. When he stole something, his mother said, there seemed little question he would be caught. It was as if he wanted to be caught, "as if he were crying out for help."

Bertilson's family went through great agony during the last decade of his life. Said his father, "We cried and we prayed. We prayed and we cried. We sometimes wondered where God was."

I last saw Bertilson in December, when he was seeking those signatures for the card he would send to the hostages. We managed to recognize one another. We spent some time talking about the good old days, and he told me he wasn't playing baseball anymore. When we parted, I made a mental note to get back to him for a status report on how he was coping with his personal demons.

Then last week, Bertilson fell down a flight of steps outside his apartment in Mankato. The fall was an accident, the coroner told the Bertilsons. Their son had fractured his skull.

Bertilson's death occurred just as it seemed he might be turning himself around. He was just a few credits from earning his degree in political science, and he had been spending a few weeks as a political science student intern with Blue Earth County.

Although he wasn't working at the time of his accident, Bertilson had been excited about his job. "He said he enjoyed it so much," his mother recalled. It was Bertilson's kind of job, his father added. "He loved people. He could work with anyone."

His parents had been excited about his new opportunity. They lived in constant hope that the best traits of their son would resurface and become dominant again, so he might ultimately find a better life.

As his father put it, "When you really love someone, it's hard to give up."

Honoring the veterans

—First published on Nov. 12, 1981

The morning sun was still low, sending long shadows from the gravestones in the LaSalle cemetery as Emil Bertilson raised the flag on the memorial to Vietnam veterans.

"Theirs was a controversial war," the Rev. Charles Beronius, interim pastor at LaSalle and Lake Hanska Lutheran churches, told about 50 people gathered for the Veterans Day ceremony. "But they served as bravely as did any other soldier in our nation's history."

A total of 57,663 U.S. soldiers died in Vietnam, and Beronius said, "We believe their lives were lost for something."

The breeze in the cemetery moved very little, and the flag remained limp at the top of the flagpole.

This flag was very special, Bertilson said. It would be flown only on special days. Another flag would be flown other days at the cemetery.

Bertilson and his wife, Bess, had decided to dedicate the flag and this monument, at the corner of the cemetery, to all Vietnam veterans—and to their son, Wayne.

Wayne Bertilson died in Mankato late in February of 1980. He was 33. He apparently had fallen down a flight of steps outside of his apartment.

He had served in Vietnam from February of 1967 to February of 1968. A member of the 9th Infantry Division, he spent most of his tour in Vietnam's Delta region.

The participants of the memorial to Bertilson and to other veterans stood still on the green lawn of the cemetery, warmed by the late autumn sun.

They sang the Star Spangled Banner, they recited the Pledge of Allegiance, and they listened to Tim Hoffman read the American Creed.

Susan Henry read a poem about wars and their wounded, Steve Graff played taps, and Rev. Beronius read from the Gospel according to St. John: "For God so loved the world…."

Willard Busse of the cemetery board accepted the monument from the Bertilsons. Mrs. Bertilson thanked those who had donated materials and talents to make the memorial a reality: Gottfried Schmiess, Floyd Blackstad, brothers Pete and Coogan Sletta, the New Ulm Monument Co.

Bertilson's parents want the monument, which stands in the same cemetery where Bertilson's body lies, to be a fitting memorial to men and women who served with their son. And, as Beronius said, "It will help us to remember a young man from our community."

The gesture by the Bertilsons in their community mirrored actions occurring in other parts of the nation.

On Veterans Day in 1982, the movement to recognize Vietnam veterans will culminate with a $7 million memorial being dedicated in Washington, D.C.

Rep. John Paul Hammerschmidt, R-Arkansas, lauded those veterans when he introduced the resolution to build the national monument, and his feelings are shared by Americans such as the Bertilsons.

"We have been struggling, as a nation," he said, "to resolve the many remaining divisions from the Vietnam war. The key to resolving Vietnam is to accord the Vietnam veteran the dignity of his experience.

"Of all the elements in this country who were involved with Vietnam, he suffered most. And of all the elements, he has received the least amount of benefits for his suffering.

"The resolution I introduce today represents a major step in showing those veterans that we, as a nation, sincerely appreciate their service. It will give every man and woman who served in Vietnam something tangible in our nation's capital, a memorial to their service and to their comrades who gave this country the ultimate gift: their lives."

A hostage comes home

—First published on Feb. 17, 1981

Saturday was Bruce Laingen's day in Odin, Minn.

He rode with wife Penne in a parade through town.

He accepted the key to the city from Mayor Larry Nordby.

He spoke to an appreciative, happy crowd of about 1,000 people, many of them Odin area residents who still remember the hometown boy.

And as the day progressed, the other famous Laingen, Arvid, seemed pleased to just sit and watch all the attention being focused upon his brother. He proved the perfect complement to Bruce, the former charge d'affaires being feted with such enthusiasm.

If no one has said it yet, it's time someone did.

Arvid Laingen has been incredible.

Through the entire hostage crisis in Iran, and through the aftermath, he has been sensitive, thoughtful, intelligent, well-spoken, cordial and patient.

Long after most of us would have tossed all those reporters out of our homes and into the shrubs, he continued to patiently answer the questions. He didn't mind at all, "even when the phone was ringing off the wall," he insisted Saturday.

"It was just the opposite. We were always so grateful Bruce was on the minds of the people."

The "prayers and attention" given to Bruce and the entire Laingen family were especially appreciated, Arvid said. "From the bottom of our hearts, thank you."

Arvid spoke to an audience Saturday that just moments earlier had listened to his brother.

Bruce had kidded Arvid about his almost daily dealings with the press, calling him "the Walter Cronkite of Odin." And Bruce had tried to pin a large bow-tie-shaped yellow ribbon on Arvid, saying he had pulled it down from its spot at the Odin Feed Mill.

Butterfield-Odin School Board Chairman Floyd Johnson told Arvid about his granddaughter discovering that one of her favorite television programs was being preempted by a special report on the hostages. Said the granddaughter: "I'm getting tired of that Arvid and his brother."

Odin State Bank President Robert Harder noted that a special sign had been put up in Odin: "Plains, Ga., has Jimmy and Billy, but Odin has Bruce and Arvid." Observed Harder: "That gives Arvid a pretty hard act to follow."

When the former hostages first returned home, Harder continued, Arvid traveled to Washington, D.C., to welcome Bruce. An official there, noting that Arvid was the brother of the former hostage, asked him if he, too, had had experience in foreign affairs. After a long pause, Arvid answered, "Well, I once test-drove a Japanese car."

When Arvid stepped to the microphone at the Odin celebration, he acknowledged that he had been warned he was going to be called upon for a few words.

However, he had kept so busy on this day, he said, that he hadn't had time to prepare a speech.

"But then," he noted, "Billy wasn't much of a speaker, either."

And regardless, Arvid said, he knew Bruce would be a tough act to follow.

The parade through Odin had been impressive, Arvid said. Earlier this year, he had been "so impressed with that ride in Washington to the White House. But, really, this was just as good as that."

Arvid said he knew that people had become tired of seeing him on television, of hearing him on the radio and of having to view "my broken-down feed mill."

He understood he would be free of that kind of attention now, but, he added, he had to express his "thanks to the media. I forgot to thank you for all the free publicity."

He joked that just as Billy Carter had Billy Beer, brewed by Cold Spring Beverages, he was working on a deal with Northland Beverages in Mankato to endorse Sun-Drop "or something like that."

When he had completed his talk, Arvid was presented with a Vigorina feed cap. He had to wear that cap, Harder said, because by now no television viewer knows him without it.

Bruce Laingen paid a high compliment when he noted Arvid's shaving-cream commentary on the day the hostages were released. Using a can of shaving cream, Arvid had written "Amen" on the window of the Odin Feed Mill.

That said it all, Bruce observed.

Bruce also promised that neither he nor Arvid would develop swelled heads because of all the attention they have attracted during the past year.

"You know, those of us who grew up in Odin and Butterfield and St. James," he said, "our heads aren't turned very easily."

With the way he handled himself during the entire crisis, Arvid demonstrated that as well as anyone.

She met Jimmy Carter

—First published on Feb. 12, 1980

The modest white house stands along Main Street in Blue Earth, Minn., just a few blocks from the downtown.

"There's a little dirt drive leading up to the side door," Susan Eisele has explained over the telephone. "Just knock on the door, and I should hear you."

So you knock, you hear some rustling inside, and eventually the door opens.

The first thing you notice is the brightly colored scarf wrapped around the woman's gray hair. Then you focus on the blue eyes that brighten as Mrs. Eisele invites you inside.

As you step into the home, your eyes wander and you see boxes and more boxes, all filled with items donated to Catholic missions—the boxes line the walls of the porch, the kitchen and the living room. Mrs. Eisele leads you along a narrow path between the boxes, along a winding path from her door to the living room, to a table and a typewriter stand where she does her writing.

"I don't know if I can tell you anything worth printing," she says. "I think I've had a little too much publicity lately." She says that because her son, Al Eisele, has been named press secretary for Walter Mondale, and Walter Mondale is the vice president for President Jimmy Carter.

"I worry about them," she says. "He [Al] says I'm silly to worry. But I'm just afraid there'll be an assassination attempt and they'll all be hurt."

She pauses, then speaks again about her son—some people may view him as a "glorified chore boy." But, she observes, Al is content to stay in the background and do his job.

"He just loves it," she says.

Susan Eisele at age 82 has gained a large measure of fame on her own, both as a news writer and as a columnist.

She has reported Blue Earth news for many years for area newspapers and radio stations. She has written a wide variety of columns for both secular and religious publications. And she still writes her popular "Countryside" column for *The Blue Earth Post.*

Even with her popularity, however, Mrs. Eisele insists that her husband, Albert, was the better writer.

"My husband was well-known as a writer, especially for short stories, both here and in Europe. He was the intellectual in the family."

Mrs. Eisele obtained her first reporting job at age 13, and she wrote her first column in 1933. Published in *The Fairmont Sentinel,* it was called "With a Penny Pencil."

In 1935, a reader sent one of her columns, entitled "Threshing Day," to the *Country Gentleman Magazine.* (The magazine later became the *Farm Journal.*)

This particular column described an action-filled day of threshing on the Eiseles' farm near Blue Earth. Based upon that column, the magazine named Mrs. Eisele the top country columnist of the year in the United States.

She was "pregnant with Al when Major Nelson, publisher of *The Sentinel,* came out to our farm to tell me about the award."

Her husband convinced her to accept the award and to take the trips that came with it—to New York City and to Washington, D.C. So, in 1936, with infant Al in her arms and a nurse by her side, she left by train for New York City.

After being wined and dined at the Waldorf-Astoria and meeting Mayor Henry La Guardia, columnist Westbrook Pegler, columnist Walter Winchell and other notables, she traveled on to Washington.

There the Eisele contingent stayed at the Mayflower Hotel, then considered "the place to be," right around the corner from the White House.

On the first morning there, Mrs. Eisele's nurse "took Al out in the perambulator, went by the White House, and found the gate was open.

"So they rolled in through the gate. She rolled Al right up onto the front porch." A couple of guards soon stopped the nurse and explained that she could not be on the White House porch.

"That was Al's first visit to the White House," Mrs. Eisele says. "We've always kidded him about that."

Susan Eisele's home has long been a collection point for donations for Catholic missions.

The donations began pouring in after Mrs. Eisele solicited them in columns she was writing for a couple of Catholic publications.

Now, she says, "I can't stop them. I've even had some brought in by helicopter."

Mrs. Eisele's first mission effort was an appeal for rosaries. She began collecting them when another son, who was studying for the priesthood, asked her to send him some broken rosaries; he and others at his seminary would repair them.

Her effort was so typically successful, with rosaries flooding in, that the bishop told her son, "For goodness sakes, tell your mother to stop sending us those rosaries."

The mission efforts slowed for awhile when Mrs. Eisele was hit by a car two years ago.

"I threw myself out of the way, or I would have been killed," she says.

Doctors who worked to save her later told Mrs. Eisele that her heart had stopped beating twice. "They had a hard time bringing me back around."

Though she still finds it somewhat difficult to walk, Mrs. Eisele has recovered most of her strength.

Having a son close to the power in Washington, D.C., has produced some exciting moments.

Mrs. Eisele greatly enjoys visiting the capital city. On her very first visit, she says, she "loved Washington. And I still do. I think it's the holy city."

On her most recent visit, Mrs. Eisele was able to visit the White House, see her son's office, and visit the office of Vice President Walter Mondale.

During her conversation with the vice president, Mondale said to her, "I have a friend who wants to meet you. His name is Jimmy."

Mrs. Eisele says she thought it was "some young fellow from Blue Earth, someone I should know."

When she walked into the room and there was President Jimmy Carter, "I almost fell over."

She's a "rabid Democrat," Mrs. Eisele says. "I just love Mr. Carter, and I'm sticking with him."

Seeing Carter in person didn't really influence her thinking on political affiliation. Such a face-to-face meeting, she smiles, well, it's just incidental.

"I've never really gone after things like that," Mrs. Eisele says. "I just like ordinary people. They're good enough for me."

Christmas poetry

—First published on Dec. 18, 1979

When Florence Hynes Willette's first book came out 21 years ago, her poems drew deep praise from Msgr. L. G. Ligutti, then editor of the Catholic *Columbia Magazine.*

"These lovely Christmas poems," the monsignor called them. "Each is a meditation, each a prayer."

Mrs. Willette's poetry, Msgr. Ligutti said, does not focus on "the splendor of distant stars, the majesty of symphonic music, of angelic choirs or prophetic voices."

Rather, "the world is made up of little things and little people, and these Christmas love notes extol the humble, enhance the trifling, while paying tribute to the Most High."

Mrs. Willette's first book, called *a handful of straw,* was published in April of 1958.

But Mrs. Willette's Christmas pieces date back much further than that. In 1943 she put together a poem for her family's Christmas cards, to be mailed to friends and relatives. She has written a poem for the cards each Christmas since, although this year she is saying, "I've got material for next year, but that may be the last year, I think."

This grand poet in the country is married to Donald Willette, best known for his Willette Seed Farms just south of Delavan, Minn.

Mrs. Willette, age 79, says they are "basically retired" now. They still live on the home farm, however, surrounded by the hectic activity of the seed farm, now operated by three of their sons. They have two other sons, a daughter, and 34 grandchildren.

Willette says his wife's writing of poems hasn't altered his life a lot. "The only impact on me—people know me as Mr. Florence Hines Willette."

Mrs. Willette's deep roots in her family and their rural life have affected her greatly. As one critic wrote of Mrs. Willette's work, it is "strong, beautiful, yet rhythmically simple poetry that speaks of love in families and friends, nature, the

Midwestern landscape and death with the surety and closeness and thorough understanding."

Mrs. Willette says she still can recall "the first poetry I wrote in country school. They were having a contest in Blue Earth or something. It was just an instinct—it was in me."

In the early 1940s, it was Msgr. Ligutti who first convinced Mrs. Willette to write some poetry for his *Columbia Magazine,* published by the National Catholic Rural Life Conference, based in Des Moines, Iowa.

In 1969, Mrs. Willette wrote a second book of poems, *Shadows and Light.*

Now a publisher from St. John's College at Collegeville near St. Cloud wants to put together a third book. The idea is to put the best of Mrs. Willette's poetry into a single volume. Her daughter Mary "told me about it," she says, "but I've just been too lazy" to compile all her works yet.

Mrs. Willette's poems have appeared in *The New York Times, The Oregonian, Columbia Magazine,* and *Spirit.* She has won a number of prizes for her work.

And while she says of her poems, "I've got a million of them—I like them all," Mrs. Willette will admit she greatly enjoys her Christmas poetry. "It's special. It's tradition. I've done it for so long it's a habit. The words just pop into my head. Sometimes I'll wake up at night with a thought—and then you work it into something."

Again this year, daughter-in-law Joanne, son Michael's wife, provided the artwork for the Willettes' Christmas cards, as she has done for a number of years.

The Willettes each year send out about 300 cards.

Their Christmas card this year features a poem Mrs. Willette calls "First Christmas Carol":

As night came down, the Star thrust forth its ray
And pointed to a stable small and old.
Good Joseph, seeing, left the traveled way
And found frail shelter from the dark and cold

He shaped a bed of straw for Mary's rest;
And there, as darkness fled from dawning's gold,
As Satan raged and heaven leaned and blessed,
Was born the Child long promised and foretold.

They rested, Joseph, Mary, Babe new-born.
Above them on a rafter perched a dove,

And suddenly, on that first Christmas morn,
It sang a glorious song of praise and love.

The music flowed and trembled on the air.
Mary and Joseph woke and smiled to hear it;
Thrilled by its loveliness, quite unaware
The rapturous singer was the Holy Spirit.

The Star of Bethlehem

—First published on Dec. 23, 1980

Now when Jesus was born in Bethlehem of Judea in the days of Herod the king, behold, there came wise men from the east to Jerusalem, saying, Where is he that is born King of the Jews? For we have seen his star in the east, and have come to worship him.

—Matthew 2, verses 1, 2

■

The year is 7 B.C., and the planets Jupiter and Saturn are poised over Judea to join the sun in a spectacular early-morning celestial show.

Near dawn on April 12, Jupiter and Saturn can be seen quite close together, just above the horizon. They remain visible in the sky only a few minutes. Then the sun moves up beneath them, and its bright rays erase stars and planets from the new day.

While resting in the morning sky, Jupiter and Saturn have appeared in the constellation Pisces (the Fishes). That is significant—to Jewish astrologers, the Pisces position in the zodiac signifies the House of the Hebrews, the ancestry of Christ.

The early-morning appearances of Jupiter and Saturn, followed closely by the sun (called a heliacal rising), soon will take on even more importance. By May 27, Jupiter and Saturn have moved into conjunction, appearing as one bright planet in the sky; then they slowly drift apart again.

Twice more during 7 B.C., Jupiter and Saturn will move together and appear in conjunction in the sky.

The triple conjunction of Jupiter, the "Star of the King," and Saturn, the "Star of the Messiah," is rare—and far more rare following a heliacal rising. It is a highly symbolic event for Jewish astrologers: it signals the coming of the Messiah. The two planets are the Star of Bethlehem.

■

Karlis Kaufmanis, professor emeritus of astronomy at the University of Minnesota and a former professor of astronomy at Gustavus Adolphus College in St. Peter, brings that message to his audience each Christmas season.

Kaufmanis's lecture, entitled "The Star of Bethlehem," has grown so popular that he has delivered it more than 800 times, and he is writing a book on the subject.

Kaufmanis is not the first astronomer to suggest that the Star of Bethlehem was really the conjunction of Jupiter and Saturn.

Johnannes Kepler, a German astronomer, first advanced the theory in the 1600s.

Kaufmanis, however, presents the idea with such great flair. It's his delivery of the message, his technique in presenting the evidence, that makes Kaufmanis so entertaining—and so effective.

"During the second conjunction, on Oct. 5, 7 B.C.," Kaufmanis says in the heavy accent of his native Latvia, "the two planets Saturn and Jupiter came so close to each other that they may have appeared like one giant star in the October sky.

"Jupiter and Saturn in *fish.* It must have been a tremendous show."

■

O morning stars, together
Proclaim the holy birth,
And praises sing to God the King
And peace to men on earth.

—From O Little Town of Bethlehem

"The writer of that verse didn't say evening star," Kaufmanis observes. "He didn't just say star. He said morning star. The heliacal rising."

Kaufmanis offers some even stronger evidence.

St. Matthew, he says, used the word "anatolai" when referring to east in "wise men from the east"; but he used "anatole" when referring to east in "his star in the east." Anatolai means east; but anatole can mean either east or "heliacal rising," Kaufmanis says. "If the writer means east in both cases, why would he not just use 'anatolai' both times?"

Then the strongest evidence of all.

Astronomers, using ancient sky records, have verified that Jupiter and Saturn did appear in conjunction three times in the year 7 B.C., during the exact period scholars now say Jesus was born—between 8 B.C. and 4 B.C.

Kaufmanis believes those conjunctions occurred on May 27, Oct. 5 and Dec. 1.

Furthermore, Kaufmanis says, Jewish astrologers who lived in Babylonia would have been watching for just such a sign.

After the heliacal rising, each conjunction would have led the wise men ("poor, plain astrologers," Kaufmanis suggests) toward Jerusalem. The wise men "postponed their journey for the cooler months of fall," and began the 500-mile trip when they saw the second conjunction, on Oct. 5, Kaufmanis says.

Then, at Jerusalem, "a miracle happened. The star they had seen in the heliacal rising was in the sky again. It led them until it stood over the birthplace of the child."

Bethlehem stands on two hills, overlooking a valley. As the wise men moved southwest toward the city, they found themselves in that valley; to them, Kaufmanis says, it would appear that the "star was resting just above the city, right over where the child was."

Since the birth of Jesus, Kaufmanis says, the same celestial show has occurred only twice, once in 799, and once again in 1464. It is expected to occur the next time in the 23rd century.

The story of the Star of Bethlehem has long endured as a symbol of our Christmas celebration, and the Jupiter-Saturn conjunction is the most widely accepted theory.

But Kaufmanis says it may never be known for sure what produced the star. As he puts it: "Only the Lord knows if my story is a correct one."

Michael Larson has collaborated on a number of books with Jill Larson Sundberg. These books include:

My Red Hat
My Red Hattitudes
Babes Remember
Cozy Cozy
Sunday Drives

Information about all of these books is available from:

Access Marketing
11025 Irwin Ave. S.
Bloomington, MN 55437
1-320-252-7679

978-0-595-83417-4
0-595-83417-5

Printed in the United States
50858LVS00004B/31-78

9 780595 834174